NO COMPROMISE

Plate 1, page 22: Womb Collection, by Eero Saarinen, 1948 (Florence Knoll Basset papers, Archives of American Art, Smithsonian Institution)

Plate 2, page 32: Knoll Bassett House 2, Cambridge, Vermont, by
Florence Knoll, circa 1980s–90s (Florence Knoll Basset papers,
Archives of American Art, Smithsonian Institution)

Plate 3, page 32: Antique capstan from a ferry boat used as a table base, Knoll Bassett House 2, Cambridge, Vermont, by Florence Knoll, circa 1980s–90s (Florence Knoll Basset papers, Archives of American Art, Smithsonian Institution);

Plate 4, page 62: Evening dress paste-up, by Loja Saarinen, 1935 (Florence Knoll Basset papers, Archives of American Art, Smithsonian Institution)

Plate 5, page 68: Drawing for dormitory at Cranbrook Academy of Art, by Florence Knoll, circa 1930s (Florence Knoll Basset papers, Archives of American Art, Smithsonian Institution)

Plate 6, page 182: Glass House, São Paulo, Brazil, by Lina Bo Bardi,
1949–52 (© Inigo Bujedo Aguirre)

Plate 7, page 128: Drawing of reception areas, Columbia Broadcasting Systems (CBS) Offices, New York, by Florence Knoll/Knoll Planning Unit, 1964 (Florence Knoll Basset papers, Archives of American Art, Smithsonian Institution)

Plate 8, page 78: Knoll Showroom, Los Angeles, by Florence Knoll/
Knoll Planning Unit, photograph by Yuichi Idaka, 1953 (Courtesy
of Knoll Archives)

Plate 9, page 116: Employees' lounge area, Connecticut General Life Insurance Company Offices, Hartford, interior design by Florence Knoll/ Knoll Planning Unit, architecture by Skidmore, Owings and Merrill, circa 1950s (Florence Knoll Basset papers, Archives of American Art, Smithsonian Institution)

Plate 10, page 159: Handwoven wool textile sample, by Evelyn Hill Anselevicius, circa 1955–62 (Philadelphia Museum of Art Archives/ Gift of Evelin Hill Anselevicius, 1983-42-16)

Plate 11, page 161: Knoll textile samples, circa 1950s (Florence Knoll Basset papers, Archives of American Art, Smithsonian Institution)

NO COMPROMISE
THE WORK OF FLORENCE KNOLL

ANA ARAUJO

Princeton Architectural Press | New York

CONTENTS

Fig. 1: Florence Knoll in Eero Saarinen's Grasshopper Chair 1950 (Courtesy of Cranbrook Archives, Cranbrook Center for Collections and Research)

INTRODUCTION

"No compromise, ever."[1] That was one of Florence Knoll's (1917–2019) most renowned statements. And indeed, one might think, why would a woman who was described by the *New York Times* as "the single most powerful figure in the field of modern design" ever need to compromise?[2]

Florence Knoll's achievements were countless. In 1961, she was awarded the Architects Gold Medal for Industrial Design from the American Institute of Architects—the first woman in the industrial design field to receive this award. In 1962, she received the Furniture Prize from the American Institute of Interior Designers. In 1977, she was given the Total Design Award from the American Society of Interior Designers. In 1979, she received an honorary degree of Doctor of Fine Arts from the Parsons School of Design.[3] And there were many more. In an industry where women are still underrepresented, Knoll stands out as a role model for the wide recognition she received and for the high standards she set. Her iconic work and career remain a source of inspiration to designers today. (Fig. 1)

Florence Knoll was best known for her work at Knoll Associates, one of the most prestigious and important furniture companies of the twentieth century, which she co-owned with her first husband and business partner Hans Knoll (1914–55).[4] Florence Knoll acted as design director for nearly

Fig. 2: Platner Collection, by Warren Platner, 1966 (Courtesy of Knoll Archives)

twenty years—from 1946 until 1965. And, for a shorter period, from 1955 to 1960, she was also the president of the company. Knoll Associates became famous for the development, production, and licensing of some of the most iconic furniture of the twentieth century: the 1929 Barcelona Chair by Mies van der Rohe (1886–1969), the 1953 Diamond Chair by Harry Bertoia (1915–78), the 1948 Womb Collection and the 1957 Pedestal Collection by Eero Saarinen (1910–61), and the 1966 Platner Collection by Warren Platner (1919–2006), to name but a few. (Plate 1, Fig. 2) During Florence Knoll's years at the company, it also had an interiors department, the Knoll Planning Unit, which concentrated on the design of workspaces, and a textile division, Knoll Textiles.[5] Florence Knoll was responsible for overseeing the production of all three departments, as well as of graphics and marketing.

Fig. 3: Textile samples as invented by Florence Knoll, circa 1955-60
(Courtesy of Knoll Archives)

She was smart and strategic: she proudly remembered
coming up with the idea of writing the word *Knoll* on the top
of the company's delivery trucks, so the name could be spot-
ted from the windows of tall buildings. And she also became
known for having invented the practice of folding a piece of
cardboard around a three-inch square of fabric and stapling
them together as a means to create a textile sample—
a procedure that is now standard in the industry. (Fig. 3) She
didn't, however, have the sense of humor of some of her male
colleagues. Her staff recalls that she hated the legendary
Knoll ad that showed a filthy chimney sweeper sitting on a
pristine Womb Chair (1948, by Eero Saarinen). While it tried
to humorously promote the robustness and practicality of
the company's products, Florence Knoll felt the joke was not
dignified.[6]

Apart from acting as design director for all creative divisions
of Knoll Associates, Florence Knoll also designed furniture
and interiors for the company. She was unassuming about her
furniture designs. "Meat and potatoes," is how she described

Fig. 4: Examples of furniture by Florence Knoll, circa 1950s (Courtesy of Knoll Archives)

them: background complements to the more sculptural pieces of designers such as Harry Bertoia and Eero Saarinen.[7] (Fig. 4)

She was more assertive with regards to her role as an interior designer, through which she created the Knoll look, understood by some to be "as much a symbol of modern architecture as Tiffany glass was a symbol of the architecture of Art Nouveau."[8] Florence Knoll's main goal was not to create a signature or to make a name for herself. It was, rather, to propagate a trend: a visual style as well as a way of working. An article in *Architectural Forum* from 1957 argued that the Knoll look could "be specified by the architect, copied by the decorator and calculated by the efficiency expert." It continued, "This is exactly what Florence and Hans Knoll intended."[9] When the Knoll Planning Unit closed in the early 1970s, some argued that the department was no longer needed, as the Knoll trend had by then been widely disseminated: "The Planning Unit's 'Knoll identity' became the standard for contemporary offices, as the design of office interiors evolved into a formalized discipline, incorporating the principles conceived by Florence Knoll."[10]

Knoll maintained that the secret for producing good design was to identify "what the problem was."[11] In a letter of congratulations for one of the awards she received, one of her colleagues stated that "without appropriate furnishings, many of today's best buildings would be empty shells."[12] To find the appropriate furnishings for the modern building: that was one of the problems Florence Knoll identified and diligently responded to. "We were not decorating," wrote one of her collaborators. "We were striving to create a new design language consistent with our times, materials, and processes, always keeping in mind that the most important part of the equation was the human being."[13]

Focusing on the interior, Florence Knoll created her own version of modernism. Her style—consistent with her architectural training from mentors such as Eliel Saarinen (1873–1950) and Mies van der Rohe and influenced by colleagues such as Charles Eames (1907–78) and Ray Eames (1916–88)—combined the boldness and sleekness of the "steel-and-glass aesthetic" with a "humanized" application of "colour, texture and comfort."[14] (Fig. 5) Florence Knoll's designs were nearly as minimal as Mies's buildings and interiors. And yet, they felt cozier and more tactile, owing these warmer qualities to the influence of Eliel Saarinen, the Eames couple, and others. Knoll's interiors combined visual precision with material fuzziness, calibrating these qualities in response to the particularities of each program, site, and client.

Florence Knoll "may have done more to promote modernism than any other woman or man," architecture author Fred A. Bernstein noted in the obituary he wrote for her in

Fig. 5: Director's office at *Look Publications* Offices,
New York, by Florence Knoll/Knoll Planning Unit, circa 1962
(Courtesy of Knoll Archives)

early 2019.[15] It was largely thanks to her that Knoll Associates went from being one of many producers and distributors of international style furniture to becoming a leading force in the market and culture of modernism. There were, of course, other companies specializing in modernist furniture during the period Florence Knoll was active. Hermann Miller, Artek, Cassina, Kartell, and Vitra were some of the best known. None, however, operated with the holistic vision of the Knoll enterprise, combining the production and licensing of furniture and furnishings with an interior design service under one roof.[16] "When I came to the company, the Planning Unit was started, because that's what I did: design," Florence Knoll said in an interview.[17] Offering a comprehensive design service was one of the factors that made Knoll Associates attractive to its clients and collaborators. "It was convenient to have it all in one place," wrote Gordon Bunshaft (1909–90), partner of the architecture firm Skidmore, Owens & Merrill.[18]

Some of Florence Knoll's interiors became iconic. These include the offices of Columbia Broadcasting Systems, General Motors, Connecticut General, H. J. Heinz, Look Publications, Alcoa, First National Bank of Miami, and Southeast Bank. Others, such as the Center for Advanced Study in the Behavioral Sciences in Palo Alto, California, were less celebrated (if, in some ways, equally innovative). (Fig. 6) Each, in its own way, helped propagate the Knoll look. In the process, these interiors demonstrated that the modern vocabulary could be "varied to produce environments with almost any pitch, with separate personalities."[19]

Together with the Knoll look came a new way of working. Informed by the modernist rationale, it involved a rigorous set of procedures that departed radically from the way interiors were conceived before that time but which the interior designer of today will recognize. In 1964, Florence Knoll wrote in an entry for *Encyclopaedia Britannica*, "The interior

Fig. 6: Study room at the Center for Advanced Study in the Behavioral Sciences, Stanford, interior design by Florence Knoll/Knoll Planning Unit, architecture by Wurster, Bernardi and Emmons, photograph by Arthur Siegel, 1955 (*Architectural Forum*, 1955)

designer's work includes programming, space planning, relation of design to mechanical equipment, selection of materials and colour, furniture design and placement and, finally, selection of art objects and accessories."[20] She played a crucial role in reshaping the field of interior design, explaining that the interior designer was a "new kind of professional…an expert consultant who understands and is in sympathy with modern architectural problems and solutions, and who is able to interpret the architect's and client's intentions and translate these into functional and pleasant spaces in which to work."[21]

Before Knoll, the professional in charge of interiors— usually known as *interior decorator* rather than *interior designer*—had no special commitment to matching the style of the building or interpreting the architect's intentions. Knoll paired interiors with architecture, and in so doing she both defined a clearer brief for the interior design profession and elevated its social and cultural status.

> While working in fields traditionally associated with the "femi-nine," such as interior design and textile design, she questioned and redefined the designations architect, interior designer and interior decorator. Knoll's working method equated the impor-tance of interior design with the building's architecture.[22]

Florence Knoll's legacy remains an exceptional contribution of a woman to the predominantly masculine world of main-stream modernism.[23] Hers was a robust, solid body of work, born from a willingness to fully engage with modernist pre-cepts. But also, importantly, it took over a niche that was, at the time, largely neglected by architects. "Interior archi-tecture," we read in an 1966 article from *Architectural Record*, "while more limited in scope than building design, requires attention which the architect, who may wish to work upon a broad canvas, will not necessarily give to this branch of his art."[24] Rather than trying to compete on equal footing with her male colleagues for a position in architecture, Knoll spot-ted a career opportunity in a much less contested field. This, together with other factors, enabled her to work for exceptional clients and develop a consistent language, which, in turn, elevated her contribution to the league of the canonical. (Fig. 7)

Her career at Knoll Associates was, however, relatively short, spanning just over two decades. After her resignation in 1965, Florence Knoll continued to work for private com-missions, consisting mainly of houses for herself and for her second husband, Miami banker Harry Hood Bassett (1917–91). In this new period of her life, Knoll finally got the opportunity to design buildings and not only their interiors. Her work from

Fig. 7: Florence Knoll (center), Frazar Wilde, and others at a conference at Connecticut General Life Insurance Company, Bloomfield, circa 1955 (Florence Knoll Basset papers, Archives of American Art, Smithsonian Institution)

this phase showed a lighter visual language—less modernist and orthodox than the Knoll look. (Plates 2, 3)

While working for Knoll Associates, the most iconic interiors Florence Knoll designed resembled living rooms, even if most of them were located within the context of corporate, commercial, or institutional settings. "The humanized elements of a Planning Unit interior referenced domestic life rather than a formal business environment," wrote design curator and author Bobbye Tigerman.[25] We can see examples of this Knoll trend in the sets of some recently produced television series—such as *Suits* (2011–19) and *Mad Men* (2007–15)—centered around life in corporate environments.[26] Through these fictional representations, we might get an idea of the ways of life unraveled in the Knoll interior.

In *Mad Men*, we see a portrayal of the Knoll look in its own historical context: the Cold War, American Dream, US of the 1950s.[27] The office depicted in the series, which referenced Knoll's interiors in its sleek-but-soft ambiance, also provided, however, a backdrop for highly unfair and discriminatory work practices, where women were repeatedly harassed and treated inappropriately, and people from this and other disenfranchised groups were overlooked. The world the series portrays was one that, to use a quote from one of the *Mad Men* characters, gave to white men "everything and so much of it," and clearly disfavored others.[28] Was the design to blame? Was the Knoll look discriminatory?

Florence Knoll used to say that an office should reflect its occupant's personality. For the one she designed for her husband and business partner Hans Knoll, she used "light teak furniture, white walls except for the one behind his desk, which was matte black, and natural Indian-silk curtains which set off his blond hair and ruddy complexion."[29] (Fig. 8). Would a person of a different race or gender look as photogenic against a Knoll background?

Fig. 8: Hans Knoll Office at 575 Madison Avenue, New York, by
Florence Knoll/Knoll Planning Unit, photograph by Robert Damora,
1951 (Florence Knoll Basset papers, Archives of American Art,
Smithsonian Institution)

The language of modernism endorsed a culture of white,
upper-middle-class masculinity, and the Knoll look might
be thought to have amplified this even further by adding to it
a domestic touch.[30] In the *Mad Men* series, for example, the
male protagonists literally adopted their cozy-yet-sleek office
as a second home. It is clear, like in the case of Hans Knoll's
office, that they enjoyed a great sense of identification with
their workspace. They often spent the night in and frequently
they used their impressive executive suites (always equipped
with a smart bar cart and a comfortable couch) as a setting

for their secret romantic affairs. While the design seemed
to be highly successful from their point of view, it also made
the work environment unfriendly and intimidating for those
who didn't share the same privileges.

Florence Knoll inherited a loaded cultural baggage,
owing partially to her design education. This started at the
Cranbrook Educational Community in Michigan (where she
befriended the Saarinens) and ended at the Armour Institute
of Chicago (where she met Mies van der Rohe). In her gap
year she interned for architects Marcel Breuer (1902–81) and
Walter Gropius (1883–1969). Architectural modernism ran in
Knoll's veins. "It is not far-fetched to say that Florence Schust
[Knoll's maiden name] was brought up by modern architecture," wrote a reporter in a 1957 article from *Interiors* magazine.[31] With it came the contentious values it embedded.

"We were taking the Bauhaus idea of design and development and making it a profitable operation," wrote Vincent
Cafiero (b. 1930), a Knoll designer.[32]

One of the main factors that enabled the company Florence Knoll directed to make a profitable operation out of the
modernist ideas was the interior design work she developed
through the Planning Unit. The Knoll company had been in
operation for three years when she joined in 1943. It already
produced its own furniture, as well as represented textile and
furniture designers with a modernist orientation from the US
and from abroad. Even though Florence Knoll contributed
greatly to the expansion of the company's production lines,
her main role, from the start, was to help with interior design.
Hans "needed a designer to do interiors and eventually I
joined him," she wrote. "This was the beginning of the Planning Unit."[33]

The Planning Unit, Knoll's interiors department, would
eventually become the "heart and soul" of Knoll Associates.[34]
Through her designs, Florence Knoll demonstrated how

the objects produced by her firm could be optimally brought together in a unified, integrated interior. While she generally underplayed her role as a furniture designer, emphasizing instead the production of the more iconic designers who collaborated with her firm, Florence Knoll considered the interiors her most relevant contribution to the design field. The Planning Unit was also a very lucrative business for Knoll Associates. The department grew by a factor of almost ninety times from its inception in 1945 until 1951, and this was only the beginning. For the next fourteen years until 1965—the year Florence Knoll left—the projects kept coming and they only grew larger, more complex, and more prestigious.[35]

Because the Planning Unit was mainly in charge of designing work spaces, especially in corporate environments, many of Florence Knoll's clients and collaborators enjoyed a privileged socioeconomic position, and they wanted the designs they commissioned to reflect their status. As head of interiors, it was Florence Knoll's job to translate and give shape to the desires of these individuals. She did this well, although not always to the benefit of promoting equality in the expression of her visual language, or providing environments that would effectively improve working conditions.

It is important to consider nonetheless that, despite her success and pride over the work she did, working with interiors was not Florence Knoll's first career choice. She trained as an architect, and hoped to practice as one, but was led to reinvent herself in response to the limited opportunities she had as a woman trying to operate in a male-dominated field. Florence Knoll worked in difficult conditions. This might have led her to endorse the status quo in order to be able to survive professionally. Yet, as I will discuss in the following lines and later in this book, a more nuanced reading of her work also reveals a will to challenge, if timidly, the "rules" she apparently abided to.

"Good design is good business," was Florence Knoll's entrepreneurial creed.[36] It proved to be effective. The business model of Knoll Associates was driven by design thinking. The company was committed to experimentation in the design as well as in the manufacturing of its products. Through an intelligent communication strategy, it won over clients and staff to its ambitious and unusual project.

Knoll Associates was unapologetic about its mistakes, inevitable when experimentation is the driving force. And it was proud of its obstinate allegiance to its own principles. In 1964, the company released an advertisement that showed a letter exchanged with one of its textile suppliers. It read:

Dear Sir, Thank you for your letter of the 6th of October which we have received today. Please be assured that we have not forgotten about you. We have only one weaver making this cloth. He is rather more of an artist than a practical man and he has an artist's temperament. In other words he makes the colour that he wants to make and not necessarily the colours we want to have from him, and if it is a nice day he will go fishing or shooting leaving the weaving for another day. You will agree that this is not very business-like and from our point of view it is impossible, but the fact is that if we want this cloth, which we do very much, we just have to put up with it. From past experience we would say that it is no use asking him to submit patterns of his future colourings as he will be unable to tell us what these are to be. The sort of thing that happens is that we get a letter from him saying that yesterday he saw a piece of rock covered with Lichen in a most beautiful colour. Sure enough in a few weeks we will get a Brown/Green mixed tweed of this colouring and this is what we mean when we say that he is an artist rather more than a weaver. With the colder winter weather approaching perhaps this man will get down doing some work to keep himself warm, we can only hope.[37]

A tag under the letter said: "It's worth waiting for a good catch." The message was clear. At Knoll Associates, quality and creativity were the priorities, and they stood above business-related requirements. As a result, the company's staff reported that sometimes work felt more like doing a school project. It took more than two years of loose experimentation for Harry Bertoia to develop the Diamond Chair. The Knolls supported him all along, as employers and as friends. And there were other similar stories.

This is not to say, however, that Knoll Associates was not committed to functional demands. Knoll Textiles, for instance, was a pioneer in the production of synthetic fabrics for the contract market: sturdy, fireproof, and easy to clean (as suggested in the chimney sweeper's ad). And the Planning Unit owed part of its success to its ability to be space effective and, as a consequence, to reduce the clients' expenses. The experimental furniture of a designer like Bertoia would not get as far were it not for Florence Knoll's down-to-earth, "meat and potatoes" pieces to complement them, supplying storage, hiding services, and visually neutralizing the interior. Knoll Associates' entrepreneurial vision consisted of providing a reliable, highly professional, first-class service that also worked as a preventive counterbalance to the eventual failures resulting from the company's riskier approach to product design and manufacturing. Florence Knoll's contribution was, to a great extent, what made this possible. Her serious, no-nonsense attitude provided a fertile ground for the flourishing of the playful and lighthearted spirit of the company she directed.

Like other American postwar design enterprises, Knoll Associates sold, primarily, an image of optimism through its products. Its flagship furniture mainly, but also its textiles, communicated a notion of nearly childish amusement—as if they were the accessories of an effortless way of life. In one of

Fig. 9: Hans and Florence Knoll, photograph by Herbert Matter, circa 1950s (Courtesy of Knoll Archives)

Knoll Associates' best-known promotional images, Florence and Hans look like they are playing (Fig. 9). Many of Knoll's ads conveyed a similar mood (Fig. 10). The joyful spirit of mid-century design was influential (Fig. 11). Many design practices of the day were inspired by its innocent, young, fun, unconditionally positive attitude. Selling a promise of instant gratification, mid-century design was, however, misleading. In its obsession with happiness, it failed to address the problematic aspects of the society it both reflected and shaped.

While, in her capacity as an entrepreneur, Florence Knoll generally supported the optimist message of the Knoll brand, in the capacity of a designer she had a more reserved attitude. As architect and editor Peter Blake wrote, at Knoll Associates, Hans was the one "totally dedicated to what we used to call 'Good Design,'" while Florence "was the one with flawless taste."[38] On the one hand, Florence Knoll's highly refined and composed character lent credibility to the work and products of Knoll Associates, promoting the disingenuous approach of mid-century design. On the other hand, the collected quality of many of her own designs suggests a refusal of the blind optimism of mid-century design. As a matter of fact, sometimes even in her capacity as an entrepreneur, Florence Knoll expressed her reservations against an overtly joyful and uncritical design approach. One case in point was her previously mentioned disapproval of the chimney sweeper's ad, which derived its humor from exposing a condition of social inequality. Although this may be hard to notice at first, Florence Knoll's design vision and the design directions taken by the Knoll brand did not always converge. They were not interchangeable. This becomes even more evident at the later stages of her career, including the designs she did after leaving the company.

Sigmund Freud's psychoanalytical theory states that the negative form does not exist in the unconscious part of our

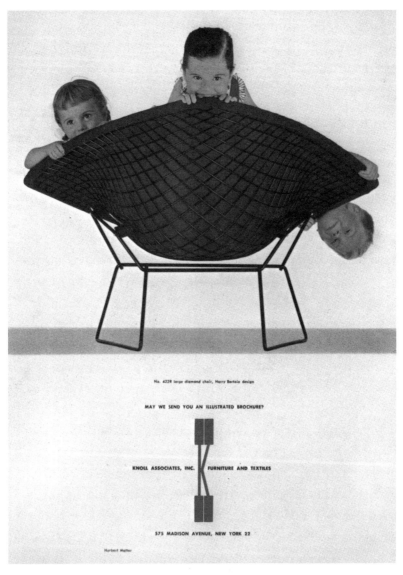

No. 422R large diamond chair, Harry Bertoia design

MAY WE SEND YOU AN ILLUSTRATED BROCHURE?

KNOLL ASSOCIATES, INC.   FURNITURE AND TEXTILES

575 MADISON AVENUE, NEW YORK 22

Herbert Matter

Fig. 10: Knoll Associates advertisement featuring the Diamond Chair by Harry Bertoia, by Herbert Matter, circa 1950s (Florence Knoll Basset papers, Archives of American Art, Smithsonian Institution)

Fig. 11: Wedding card to Florence Schust Knoll Bassett and Harry Hood Bassett, by Charles and Ray Eames, 1958, showing an innocent, optimistic, and playful approach typical of mid-century American design (Florence Knoll Basset papers, Archives of American Art, Smithsonian Institution)

minds: "There are in this system no negation, no doubt, no degrees of certainty. Negation is a substitute, at a higher level, for repression."[39] Freud argued that when we make a statement preceded by a negative—as in, "no compromise, ever"—what we might be effectively trying to say is more or less the opposite. Freud's thought is intriguing in the light of some interviews Florence Knoll gave years after her resignation from Knoll Associates. While declaring to be extremely proud of her career and achievements, she lets some comments slip that may suggest otherwise.

Far from being compromise free, Knoll's career had its fair of twists and turns. Having access to prestigious commissions and receiving wide professional recognition while working for Knoll Associates meant she had to abide to strict modernist principles and limit the scope of her work to the realm of interiors (rather than practicing as an architect according to her training). After she resigned, Knoll experimented with a freer design language and had the opportunity to act as an architect, designing two houses for herself and her partner.[40] This was, however, only due to her extremely privileged personal circumstances, and this part of her work is often not acknowledged as part of her professional achievements.

Another "negative" claim that Knoll became known for was "I am not a decorator."[41] In a 1964 interview with the *New York Times*, she added: the "only place I decorate is my own house."[42] During her career at Knoll Associates, Florence Knoll many times endorsed the hierarchy that suggested that the role of architect and the designer was culturally more relevant than the one of the decorator—a claim that indirectly reinforced a discriminatory professional ranking based on gender difference (for decoration was, at the time, a profession largely associated with women and with a feminine sensibility). Who would think that, after leaving Knoll Associates in

1965, Knoll would devote a considerable part of her life being, precisely, a decorator and decorating her own houses?

Most accounts of Florence Knoll tend to take her work and statements at face value, ignoring their contradictions and biases.[43] In so doing, they take the culture in which she operated for granted and sometimes fail to highlight the more nuanced aspects of the person and the professional she was. Through understanding the compromises Florence Knoll gave in to, one is able to look at her contribution from a different angle, distinguishing the aspects of her work that should be appreciated for their historical worth only from the aspects that remain valuable and inspiring from the point of view of our own contemporary design culture.

NOTES

1. Mel Byars, "Florence Knoll: 'No Compromise'" *Graphis* 312 (1997): 97–99.
2. Virginia Lee Warren, "Woman Who Led an Office Revolution Rules an Empire of Modern Design," *New York Times*, September 1, 1964, 40.
3. See "Awards," Florence Knoll Bassett Papers, Archives of American Art, Smithsonian Institution (Series 7).
4. Florence Knoll changed her name twice during her life. She was born Florence Margaret Schust in 1917, became Florence Knoll when she married Hans Knoll in 1946, and then changed her name to Florence Knoll Bassett when she married Miami banker Harry Hood Bassett in 1958. I will use "Florence Knoll" here, as this is the name that the design world generally employs. The company she co-owned, currently named Knoll, also changed names during its history. When it was first incorporated by Hans Knoll in 1938, it was Hans G. Knoll Furniture. In 1943, the name of the company changed to H. G. Knoll Associates. When Florence officially became a partner in 1946, it became Knoll Associates. In 1950, the European operations of Knoll Associates became Knoll International. In 1959, Knoll Associates was sold to Art Metal, and in 1969 the whole company changed its name to Knoll International. In 1990, Knoll International was bought by Westinghouse Electric and grouped with other companies, becoming part of an entity named the Knoll Group. In 1995 the Knoll Group was sold to Warburg Pincus Ventures and renamed as Knoll. Some of these dates are inconsistent in different documents. The ones mentioned here are from Earl Martin, ed., *Knoll Textiles: 1945–2010* (New Haven: Yale University Press, 2011).
5. The Knoll Planning Unit was closed in the early 1970s. Today Knoll is a design group comprising eleven different divisions: Knoll Office, KnollStudio, KnollExtra, KnollTextiles, Muuto, DatesWeiser, Spinneybeck, FilzFelt, Edelman Leather, and Holly Hunt.
6. See Eric Larrabee and Massimo Vignelli, *Knoll Design* (New York: Harry N. Abrams, 1981), 106 and Brian Lutz, *Knoll: A Modernist Universe* (New York: Rizzoli, 2010), 51.
7. Larrabee and Vignelli, *Knoll Design*, 77.
8. "The Knoll Interior" (unauthored) *Architectural Forum* (March 1957), 137.
9. Ibid, 137. On the ubiquity of the Knoll look, see also Bobbye Tigerman, "'I Am Not a Decorator': Florence Knoll, the Knoll Planning Unit and the Making of the Modern Office," *Journal of Design History* 20, no. 1 (Spring 2007): 61–74.
10. Lutz, *Knoll*, 38.
11. Video interview with Florence Knoll, 1998 (Cranbrook Archives, Detroit).
12. Nembhard N. Culin of Frederick G. Frost Jr. & Associates Architects to Florence Knoll, April 26, 1961, in "Awards," Folder 10, 19.
13. Lutz, *Knoll*, 32.
14. Tigerman, "Not a Decorator," 61.
15. Fred A. Bernstein, "Florence Knoll Bassett, 1917–2019," *Architectural Record* 207, no. 3 (March 2019): 31.
16. The Hermann Miller Furniture Company, established in Michigan in 1923, was, during Florence Knoll's tenure, Knoll Associates' most important competitor. It did not, however, launch its own textile division until 1952 (Knoll's textiles date from 1947), and it started to provide interior design services only as late as 1964—one year before Florence Knoll left Knoll Associates. Artek was established in Finland in 1935. It sold modern furniture, lighting, textiles, and glassware, but provided no interior design services. Cassina was founded in Milan, Italy, in 1927. In the 1950s the company gained prominence for licensing and commissioning progressive designs by architects and designers, including Gio Ponti (1891–1979), Franco Albini (1905–77), Charlotte Perriand (1903–99), and Le Corbusier (1887–1965). Cassina has always been focused only on furniture design and production. Kartell was founded in 1949, also in Milan. It was strongly committed to "research, innovation, aesthetics, and quality," and it "did much to change attitudes to everyday domestic products made in plastic." (Jonathan M. Woodman, *Oxford Dictionary of Modern Design* [Oxford: Oxford University Press, 2004], 236, s.v. "Kartell."). It did not provide furnishings and contract services until 1963. Vitra was founded in Switzerland in 1950. It has licensed furniture from Hermann Miller since 1957, and, from its beginnings, it has focused on product design rather than on furnishings or interiors. While Florence Knoll's company pioneered on many fronts, it was also strongly influenced by other furniture businesses—especially Artek—whose products Hans Knoll sold in 1941. Knoll Associates (and Hermann Miller) may have gotten the idea of producing and selling textiles from Artek.
17. Lutz, *Knoll*, 29.
18. Larrabee and Vignelli, *Knoll Design*, 134.
19. "Office of Merit: A Humane Campus for

the Study of Man, CBS Offices by the Same Designer" (unauthored), *Architectural Forum* (January 1955): unnumbered.

20. Draft of entry for *Encyclopaedia Britannica*, s.v. "interior design," set to appear in the 1964 printing, Knoll Archives, New York (hereafter Knoll Archives).

21. Ibid.

22. Tigerman, "Not a Decorator," 62.

23. There were a few other women designers who, like Knoll, worked under the direct influence of architectural modernism. Eileen Gray (1878-1976), Lilly Reich (1885-1947), Aino Marsio Aalto (1894-1949), Charlotte Perriand (1903-99), Ray Eames (1916-88), Lina Bo Bardi (1914-92), and Alison Smithson (1928-93) were among the best known. The work of some of these designers (mainly Bardi, but also Eames and Smithson) is today categorized as eccentric, while that of others (Reich, Perriand, Aalto) is often recognized predominantly for the women's collaboration with iconic male designers. Many of these women (including Gray and Perriand) had rather patchy careers, relating greatly to the precarious opportunities that were available for them. Florence Knoll's contribution was unique in relation to the work of these women in the sense that it stood on its own and that it was smoothly assimilated by the architectural mainstream. Nevertheless, because she was operating from a furniture company rather than a conventional office, she did not become as well known as these other female designers.

24. Mildred Schmertz, "Distinguished Interior Architecture for CBS," *Architectural Record, 139* (June 1966): unnumbered.

25. Tigerman, "Not a Decorator," 69.

26. See "Matthew Weiner's *Mad Men*," Design Pulse, Inspiration, Shop & Browse, Knoll, accessed September 2, 2019, https://www.knoll.com/knollnewsdetail/Mad-Men, which lists all Knoll furniture used in the series.

27. The series starts in the 1950s and spans two decades, with its last episodes set in the 1970s. See Danielle M. Stern, Jimmie Manning, and Jennifer C. Dunn, eds., *Lucky Strikes and a Three Martini Lunch: Thinking about Television's* Mad Men (Newcastle upon Tyne: Cambridge Scholars Publishing, 2012) and Rod Carveth and James B. South, eds., *Mad Men and Philosophy: Nothing Is as It Seems* (Hoboken, NJ: John Wiley & Sons, 2010).

28. Ashley Jihee Barkman, "Mad Women," in Carveth and South, *Mad Men*, 206.

29. Larrabee and Vignelli, *Knoll Design*, 80.

30. For an analysis of the relationship of modernism with white masculinity, see Mark Wigley, *White Walls, Designer Dresses: the Fashioning of Modern Architecture* (Cambridge: MIT Press, 2001). For an analysis of its endorsement of upper-middle-class values, see Robin Schuldenfrei, *Luxury and Modernism: Architecture and the Object in Germany 1900-1933* (Cambridge: MIT Press, 2018).

31. "Florence Knoll and the Avant-Garde," (unauthored) *Interiors* (July 1957), unnumbered.

32. Larrabee and Vignelli, *Knoll Design*, 142.

33. "Biographical Material," Florence Knoll Bassett Papers, Archives of American Art, Smithsonian Institution (Series 1, Folder 1, 13).

34. Bobbye Tigerman, "The Heart and Soul of the Company: The Knoll Planning Unit, 1944-65," in Martin, *Knoll Textiles*, 178-228.

35. After Knoll left, designer Lewis Butler, who had been for long working in the Planning Unit, was appointed director of design. However, the division never again achieved the scale and scope of work it had had under Florence Knoll. In 1971, the Planning Unit was finally closed. See Tigerman, "Heart and Soul."

36. Video Interview with Florence Knoll, 1998 (Cranbrook Archives, Detroit).

37. Knoll Associates advertisement featuring letter from W. Bill of Bond Street to Knoll Associates (Knoll Archives).

38. Peter Blake, *No Place Like Utopia: Modern Architecture and the Company We Kept* (London: W. W. Norton, 1997), 172.

39. Salman Akhtar and Mary Kay O'Neil, eds., *On Freud's "The Unconscious"* (London: Karnac, 2013), 48.

40. Both houses consisted of extensions of previously existing buildings. As Florence Knoll explains, "The first house [Knoll Bassett House 1] was keyed to expand from a private area to include larger spaces for entertainment. The Vermont house [Knoll Bassett House 2] began as a temporary cottage for the family, but it expanded into three units with a tennis barn for summer and winter use." ("Biographical Material," 87).

41. Warren, "Woman Who Led Office."

42. Ibid.

43. See, for instance, Tigerman, "Not a Decorator"; Larrabee and Vignelli, *Knoll Design*; Lutz, *Knoll*; and Martin, *Knoll Textiles*.

CHAPTER ONE: FLORENCE KNOLL BEFORE KNOLL ASSOCIATES

One of the strongest memories of Florence Knoll's childhood, she recalled, was looking at blueprints on her father's desk: "They seemed enormous to a five year old, but nonetheless, I was enchanted by them."[1] This was 1922. A year later, her father, Frederick E. Schust, passed away. Perhaps out of an unconscious desire to pay tribute to him, Florence Knoll would, some ten years on, stand out as the only girl in her class at the Kingswood School for Girls to choose architecture as her main field of interest. "While other girls in Kingswood were inclined to regard the building merely as a center for the school's activities, young Schust became fascinated with the building itself."[2] By this time, her mother had also died, and she had become a boarding student at Kingswood, a part of the Cranbrook Educational Community that comprised the Cranbrook Academy of Art led by celebrated Finnish architect Eliel Saarinen.

Founded by the newspaper baron and philantropist George Gough Booth (1864–1949) and his wife Ellen Warren Scripps Booth (1863–1948) in 1927, the Cranbrook Educational Community consisted of six institutions: Brookside School Cranbrook, Cranbrook School (for boys), Kingswood School (for girls), Cranbrook Academy of Art, Cranbrook Institute of Science, and Christ Church Cranbrook. It had developed out of the owners' desire to make a contribution to the community

Left, Fig. 1: Kingswood School for Girls, Bloomfield Hills, Michigan, by Eliel Saarinen, 1931 (Florence Knoll Basset papers, Archives of American Art, Smithsonian Institution); **Right, Fig. 2:** Weaving workshop at Kingswood, circa 1930s (Courtesy of Cranbrook Archives, Cranbrook Center for Collections and Research)

by creating an environment that would foster personal development, spiritual growth, and social engagement.

The Booths bought the farm where the Cranbrook Educational Community was to be developed in Bloomfield Hills, Michigan, in 1904. In 1908 their family moved to their new home, Cranbrook House, designed by a well-known Detroit architect, Albert Khan. In 1915, they launched the first public building in the estate, the Greek Theatre, which was followed by the Meeting House, finished in 1918. When the Booths met the Saarinen family in the mid-1920s, they immediately joined forces. Eliel was invited to design several buildings in the campus and became the president of the Art Academy. His wife Loja (1879–1968) became head of the Weaving department. The Saarinens moved to the Saarinen House in

Bloomfield Hills in 1930, where Loja and Eliel would live
until 1950.

What first drew Knoll to Kingswood when she visited
in 1931 was the peculiarity of its settings. "I had heard of
Kingswood, and we went to check it out. I was enthralled by
its unique beauty and made an immediate decision that it was
the right place for me. As a result my interest in design and
future career began there."[3] (Fig. 1) Kingswood offered what
was considered at the time an innovative educational program largely based on the promotion of crafts. One of the first
activities Knoll engaged with when she entered the school
was weaving. She started to learn the craft in a workshop
supervised by Loja herself. "Loja stimulated my interest in
texture and color," she recalled.[4] (Fig. 2) The teacher who first
introduced Knoll to architectural design was Rachel DeWolfe
Raseman (1895–1984), an architect who had graduated from
Cornell University and who was the art director at Kingswood.[5] "She guided me into the world of architecture and
design," wrote Knoll. "I learned the basics of planning and
drafting and my first project was to design a house. The
project took as much time as I could spare away from my
other studies to draw the plans and elevations and make a
model."[6] (Figs. 3, 4) When Eliel Saarinen learned about the girl's
interest in architecture, he started to see her occasionally
in the capacity of a mentor. Knoll wrote, "It was during that
time that Eliel Saarinen took an interest in me and stopped by
occasionally to discuss my project."[7]

Dubbed the "country club of schools," the settings of
the Cranbrook Educational Community were idyllic and
peaceful, with "an air of separation from external pressures."[8]
"There were as many gardeners as students," Jack Lenor
Larsen (b. 1927), a New York textile designer who studied at
the Cranbrook Academy of Art in the early 1950s, jokingly
remembered.[9] The teaching practices were informal:

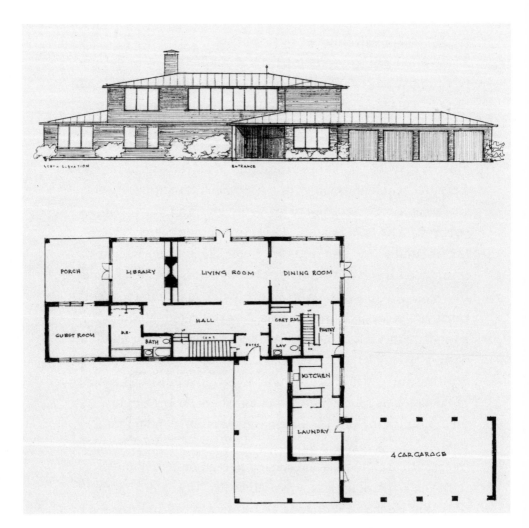

Fig. 3: Elevation and plan of Florence Knoll's first design for a house, circa 1930s (Florence Knoll Basset papers, Archives of American Art, Smithsonian Institution)

The school operated on the atelier system—students worked in groups around masters in each art and craft, pursuing their own projects under the guidance of their teachers, while acting as apprentices to those teachers at the same time. There were no classes and no grades—the notion of inspiration was all.[10]

At the Cranbrook community, students and teachers engaged as members of one big family. Practicing weaving under Loja's guidance and architecture under Eliel's and having the school as her only home as a consequence of being an orphan, Knoll was soon integrated into the Saarinen household.

The Saarinens befriended me and took me under their wing. They asked my guardian permission to accompany them to Hvitträsk (1903), their home in Finland for the summer, and summers thereafter, which always included a trip to the Continent to see interesting architecture and exhibitions.[11] (Fig. 5)

At Hvitträsk, Knoll took lessons in architectural history from her "big brother" Eero, the youngest child of Eliel and Loja.

Eero loved to draw and did so with lightning speed. He could draw in two directions at the same time, of course, with both hands. I don't know where he got his knowledge of history, but it flowed from his pens with great detail. He explained architectural and historical reasons for the development of design throughout the ages with the drawings and details emerging as he spoke in the summer of 1935 at Hvitträsk in Finland.[12] (Fig. 6)

The Saarinens played a crucial role in nurturing and guiding Florence Knoll in her vulnerable years as a teenage orphan. Apart from losing her parents at a very young age, Knoll had also witnessed the passing of her brother, Frederick, when she was only three years old. When her mother Mina

Fig. 5: Holidaying with the Saarinens: Florence Knoll with Eliel Saarinen and his grandson Bob Swanson, circa 1930s (Courtesy of Cranbrook Archives, Cranbrook Center for Collections and Research)

Matilda (née Haist) died in 1929, Knoll was put under the care of a legal guardian, banker Emil Tessin, who was a friend of the family. Knoll came from a privileged background. She was the heir of a baking business started by her Swiss-German grandfather, the Schust Baking Company, which was acquired by a national corporation—Sunshine Biscuits—in 1930. Knoll had an uncle and an aunt from her father's side, and an aunt from her mother's side (originally from Canada; Florence was named after another of her mother's sisters, deceased the year before she was born). The fact that Florence Knoll's mother chose a friend, rather than a family member, as a guardian for her daughter suggests, however, that her family links may not have been very strong. As a matter of

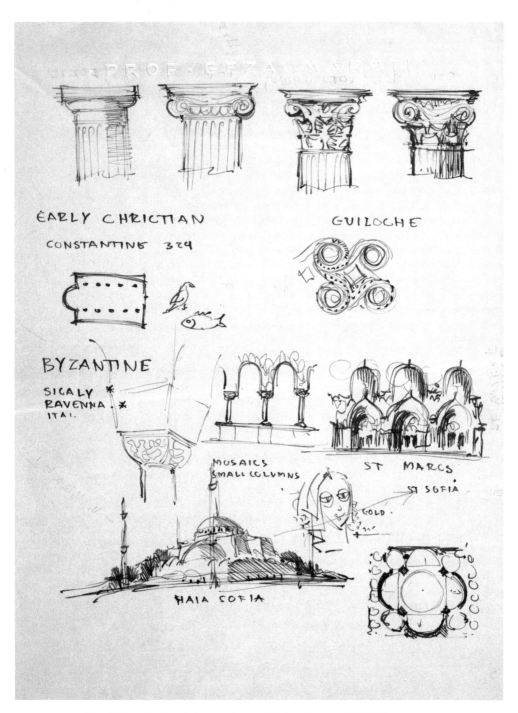

Fig. 6: Eero Saarinen's lessons in architectural history, 1935 (Florence Knoll Basset papers, Archives of American Art, Smithsonian Institution)

fact, Knoll never makes mention of any of her relatives in her collected papers—the archive she curated about her work, life, and career—or elsewhere.[13] This implies how reliant she must have been on the emotional support she received from the Saarinens.

Eliel was not only an influential mentor to Florence Knoll during the early days of her design education, he was also the architect behind the Kingswood School for Girls, the place Knoll was so "enthralled" by that she took "an immediate decision" to move there. She showed, throughout her life, an unconditional respect toward him, who played for her a double role as an inspirational professional and as an adopted parent. Knoll was also deeply attached to Loja, albeit in a different way that I will discuss later in this chapter. (Fig. 7)

One of the implications of Florence Knoll's early and very strong connection with the Saarinen family was that her character, as a designer and as a person, was greatly defined by their views and lifestyle. "Life with the Saarinens was not just work," she wrote.

> In spite of their Scandinavian reserve, they had a great sense of fun and had amusing friends and gave lively dinner parties. We made interesting trips in Finland and then on the Continent at the end of each summer. In the thirties travel was slow by boat or train. The advantage was a leisurely trip through the unexplored countryside of countries like Estonia, Latvia and Lithuania on our way to visit the Saarinens' friends in Hungary. They lived near Budapest on the Danube and entertained us royally in this beautiful area—including a trio of gypsy musicians every night at the cocktail hour.[14]

The Saarinens had arrived in the US in 1923—eight years before they met Knoll—escaping economic recession in their home country. By this time, Eliel already had an established

Fig. 7: Back: Eero Saarinen, his wife Lilian Saarinen, Florence Knoll, and Hans Knoll. Center: Eliel Saarinen and Loja Saarinen. Front: Eric Saarinen, son of Eero and Lilian, late 1940s (Courtesy of Cranbrook Archives, Cranbrook Center for Collections and Research)

Fig. 8: Kingswood School for Girls, Bloomfield Hills, Michigan, by Eliel Saarinen, 1931 (Florence Knoll Basset papers, Archives of American Art, Smithsonian Institution)

reputation as an architect, having built large projects, such as the Helsinki Railway Station (1919), as well as many smaller residential schemes, including Hvitträsk (which took its name from the idyllic lake that surrounded it).

The Kingswood School for Girls—Knoll's second home—followed similar design principles to the ones Saarinen had developed while working in Finland. He designed the school in collaboration with his wife Loja, and his children Pipsan (Eva Lisa, 1905–79) and Eero. (Fig. 8) Completed in 1931, Kingswood was the second building Saarinen did for the Cranbrook complex. (Florence Knoll was in the second class of students.) Three years earlier, he had finished the Cranbrook School for Boys, his first American project to be built.

One of the tenets Saarinen defended as a designer was the celebration of "good" craftsmanship. As a matter of fact,

his interest in crafts got him involved with the Cranbrook
project in the first place. He was introduced to George and
Ellen Booth, the patrons of the school, by their son Henry,
who was Saarinen's student at the University of Chicago. Like
Eliel, George Booth saw the return to the crafts as a means
to promote cultural and social reform. His ultimate aim was
to "banish tasteless, mass-produced goods from American
homes. He believed that craftmanship would result in superior products and provide the foundation for an ethically
responsible life."[15] Both men had been inspired by British
Arts and Crafts movement.

> Born of thinkers and practitioners in Victorian England who
> despaired the ornate clutter which seemed to be pervading
> architecture and design, [the Arts and Crafts] was a movement
> about integrity. It was about respecting your materials, and
> the way you used them. It was about showing how things were
> constructed, so that they never looked different from what they
> really were. Equally, it was about respecting the maker. Against
> a background of the filth and degradation of industrialisation,
> the Arts and Crafts Movement wanted people to work in happy,
> healthy surroundings, and to take pleasure in what they made.[16]

Like their British colleagues, Saarinen and Booth aligned the
idea of "good" craft with the notion of "honesty." "We went
back to the nature of the material and tried to find a simple
and honest way of using this material," Saarinen wrote about
his architecture.[17]

"Simple" and "honest," for Saarinen, had a practical as
well as an aesthetic connotation. On the practical side, he
praised qualities like durability and robustness, which he felt
could be better achieved in handmade and manufactured
products than in mass-produced ones. With regard to aesthetics, Saarinen, again in alignment with the Arts and Crafts

Fig. 9: Drawing for *Festival of the May Queen* tapestry, by Eliel Saarinen, 1932 (Florence Knoll Basset papers, Archives of American Art, Smithsonian Institution)

philosophy, wanted to do away with what he called "nonsensical" ornamentation.[18]

> After the ornamental sweet dreams and decorative frightfulness, the road onward seemed pretty hazy. It was a well-known fact in those days that, to pioneer, one had to be clear-headed enough to steer between the Scylla of overused classicism and the Charybdis of random forms of sparkling novelty. There were many exaggerations, many mistakes, many compromises, and many outright retreats to the old.[19]

Saarinen spoke of digging honesty out "from its ornamental grave."[20] He did not completely condemn ornamentation, as some of his modernist colleagues would do some years later. Instead, Saarinen opted to work with forms of decoration that, in his view, belonged in a building because there was a good enough reason for them to be there. In Kingswood, for example, an important decorative element was the tapestry entitled *Festival of the May Queen* (1932), located in the dining room. (Fig. 9) One of many collaborations between Eliel and Loja (he made the original drawing and she, together with her team, was in charge of the weaving), it showed a ritual that celebrated the arrival of spring. Because this ritual, often celebrated with a girls' parade, related to the program of the building (a school for girls), the decoration was, in Saarinen's view, justified.

Saarinen called his way of working "total design." As his son, Eero, explained years later:

> Perhaps the most important thing I learned from my father was that in any design problem one should seek the solution in terms of the next largest thing. If the problem is an ashtray, then the way it relates to the table will influence its design. If the problem is a chair then its solution must be found in the way it relates to the room.[21]

Total design implied that all elements in a building should be streamlined in order to articulate a single, fully coherent design language. "We did a total design," Florence Knoll also said when she described her work at Knoll Associates—"furniture, fabrics and interiors."[22] Total design translated as a pursuit of coherence, consistency, and purposefulness. Praised by many architects and designers from the early twentieth century until today, it was, compared to what had been in vogue at the time, a pretty puritanical and cerebral way of conceiving the experience of design. "Total design" relied on knowledge, as opposed to taste. It promoted honesty, in place of theatricality or fantasy. Expressing her alliance to the principle of total design, Florence Knoll noted in a 1964 interview: "I am interested only in things that are real."[23]

The intended "realism" and earnestness of Saarinen's design approach, which Knoll partially inherited, challenged

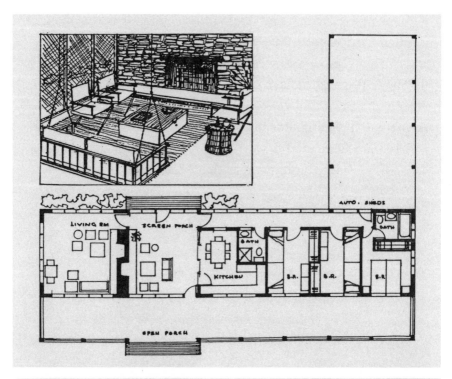

Top, Fig. 11: Interior view and plan of Michigan Summer House, by
Florence Knoll, circa 1930s (Florence Knoll Basset papers, Archives
of American Art, Smithsonian Institution); **Bottom: Fig. 10,** Sketch of
Michigan Summer House, by Florence Knoll, circa 1930s (Florence Knoll
Basset papers, Archives of American Art, Smithsonian Institution)

the freedom and exuberance of the architectural eclecticism of the nineteenth century. Most importantly for the purpose of this discussion, it also countered the understanding, widely accepted at the time, of the interior as a place to harbor "illusions." As cultural critic Walter Benjamin famously wrote of the nineteenth-century interior, "the far away and the long ago" came together.[24] Benjamin associated the interior with the world of detective novels. For him, this was a place of mystery—not objectivity—where the "traces of the inhabitant" were "imprinted."[25] Benjamin claimed that human beings needed the illusion of the interior as a means to account for their own psychological and emotional complexity. He likened the interior to a "phantasmagoria," meaning "a confused group of real or imagined images that changed quickly, one following the other as in a dream."[26]

This definition could not be further away from Eliel Saarinen's (and later Florence Knoll's) plea for consistency and sense. In the first house Knoll designed as a student at Kingswood—under Saarinen's mentorship—one notices the predominance of an objective, matter-of-fact approach. The same applies to her second student design she kept in her collected papers, this one developed when she graduated from Kingswood and became a student at the Cranbrook Academy of Art. "I was intrigued with the idea of making the screen porch the center of the house," Knoll wrote, "free from summer insects but with a feel of being outside."[27] (Figs. 10, 11) In the perspective drawing she showed of this porch, one notices the celebration of "honest" craft—in the textured surfaces and objects—as well as of total design. Evidencing her loyalty to Saarinen's principles, Knoll fitted the design elements together logically and harmoniously. The design language is rigorous and contained. There is no space for fantasy, dream, or illusion.

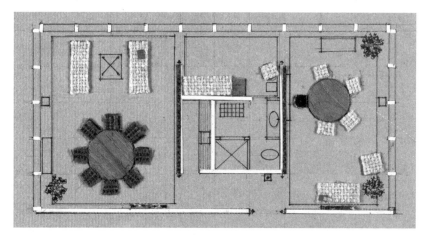

Fig. 12: Paste-up of Jack Heinz Suite at H. J. Heinz Company
Headquarters, Pittsburgh, by Florence Knoll, 1958 (Florence Knoll
Basset papers, Archives of American Art, Smithsonian Institution)

Eliel played primarily the role of a mentor for Knoll,
resulting in her early assimilation of his clear-cut design
tenets and in her commitment to the notion of total design,
which would later define her signature look. Knoll's connection with Loja was, contrarily, much more personal and
intimate than her rapport with Eliel.

> Loja Saarinen made this delightful evening dress for me in
> 1935. She made this enclosed card for Christmas and proceeded
> to make the actual dress thereafter so she could do the proper
> fittings. The skirt had the special "pleating" made by drawing
> a thread of the fabric through the material to produce the effect.
> It must have been a very exacting job, but the result was
> wonderful.[28] (Plate 4)

This card showed a type of drawing, known as a "paste-up,"
that was commonly used in clothing and set design at the
time. Knoll liked it so much that she took it as an inspiration
for her own signature style of drawing in her years at Knoll
Associates. (Fig. 12) "It was extraordinary how small swatches

of fabrics and wood could convey a feeling of the space," Knoll wrote of her own paste-ups. "I always felt the need to employ this system that eventually was used by design offices as a standard."[29] It is significant that, influenced by Loja, Knoll developed a method of representation borrowed from the fields of clothing and set design. For these were disciplines that had a natural propensity to engage a dimension of fiction and illusion not distant from Benjamin's definition of the interior. "Woman is quite within her rights," wrote French poet Charles Baudelaire when he reflected on the social and cultural role of fashion, "when she devotes herself to appearing magical and supernatural."[30] In this sense, through the use of the "paste-up" Knoll discreetly introduced in her design language some of the values that Eliel Saarinen had rejected. She did it cautiously. If Loja's card—and dress—evoked the more "magical and supernatural" domain of feminine clothing, Knoll's drawings—and interiors—often showed a more constrained vocabulary. They related to the presumably more down-to-earth language of masculine tailoring.

Knoll would, in fact, pay an even more direct tribute to tailoring in the early years of her career at Knoll Associates. Responding to the scarcity of materials during World War II, she resorted to using suiting fabrics for the upholstering of the company's first furniture pieces. "She found viable options in men's suiting fabrics in 'ranges of grey and beige flannels and tweeds from Scotland,' which she thought looked elegant on a chair and could be readily purchased in quantity from New York tailors."[31] (Fig. 13) It was safer for Florence Knoll to engage with a masculine aesthetic in her design work than to openly follow the lead suggested by Loja Saarinen's paste-up. In this way she not only avoided confronting Eliel's design principles but also averted any possibility of entangling her work with the stigma that was, at the time, associated with all things feminine, fashion included. Her choice was not, however,

Fig. 13: Chair with upholstery made of suiting fabric, by Florence Knoll, photograph by Scott Hyde, circa 1950s (Courtesy of Knoll Archives)

really about the pursuit of honesty. Male suits were, after all, also theatrical in their own way. And they were as entrenched with the fashion system as was feminine dress.

> It has been supposed that men either were relieved of their sartorial obligations through an appropriation of the activity by women, or were convinced of its unworthiness by a social doctrine which equated fashionability with feminine "vanity" or "susceptibility"; the constraining possibilities in terms of the narrower range of masculine sartorial models on offer, and an underlying insistence on the un-manliness of the whole clothing business in general, actually positioned men right at the centre of a debate concerning fashion and modern life while apparently denying their participation.[32]

Knoll's decision of abiding to a more masculine look worked conveniently as a means to articulate the evocative qualities conveyed by Loja's paste-up—and, albeit in a contrived way, continue the tradition of the nineteenth-century interior—in a manner that would not openly oppose the values defended by Eliel. (Fig. 14) It was a compromise. Remarkably, this

Fig. 14: A sitting room in the residence of interior decorator Elsie de Wolfe in New York, ca. 1895 (The Museum of the City of New York, NY, USA)

compromise worked significantly in favor of endorsing a gender-biased status quo. Florence Knoll entered the design scene at a time when women were starting to find their voices and gain professional and social recognition, particularly in the field of interiors, through the development of a language that celebrated precisely the values she chose to deride. Thanks to Eliel's influence, her aesthetic vocabulary was considerably more reduced than that of other interior decorators of her time. Whereas they allowed themselves to take inspiration from reality as well as from fantasy, from feminine as well as from masculine references, from Western as well as from non-Western sources, from an abstract as well as from a figurative vocabulary, Florence Knoll, in contrast, based her aesthetic expression on coherence and exclusion. In a context where feminine identity was associated with an unrestrained combination of influences, Knoll chose to narrow her vocabulary down to elements and procedures that posed no challenge to the prevailing rules imposed by the male-dominated mindset of the time.

Whenever she used designs elements that were foreign to the predominantly Western, masculine, and abstract language

Fig. 15: Pandanus Fabric Sample, by Knoll Textiles, 1948–50
(The Museum of Modern Art, New York, NY, U.S.A. Digital Image ©
The Museum of Modern Art/Licensed by SCALA / Art Resource, NY)

of modernism, Knoll tended to neutralize them in the name
of consistency, as established by the principle of total design.
One example was the first showroom she designed for Knoll
Associates, at 601 Madison Avenue, New York.

> Knoll, 601 Madison, was my first experience designing a
> showroom. The existing space in an old building was a simple
> rectangle with reasonable fenestration and ceiling height.
> I had become enamored by the T-bar as a structural element
> and used it to divide the space without visually blocking it.
> I used wrapped cord and open weave pandanus cloth to
> further this concept.[33]

The Pandanus Cloth was a handwoven, plant-fiber textile
imported from the Philippines. It had a notably lighter, more
fragile, and wobblier weave than the other textiles used by
Knoll in this project—a quality that evidenced its eccentric
provenance. (Fig. 15) Rather than playing with this particularity
(as an interior decorator of the time would typically have
done), Florence Knoll folded it into her general design con-
cept, counterbalancing its effect with other similarly fragile

Fig. 16: Setting with Pandanus upholstery at Knoll Showroom, 601 Madison Avenue, New York, by Florence Knoll/Knoll Planning Unit, 1948 (Florence Knoll Basset papers, Archives of American Art, Smithsonian Institution)

elements and design gestures (such as the above-mentioned wrapped cord).[34] (Fig. 17) As a consequence, this unique Pandanus Cloth became, in Knoll's intervention, virtually unnoticeable. (Fig. 16)

The coherence of Florence Knoll's design language came, most of the time, with the price of muting elements that could potentially bring more richness and diversity to the atmospheres she created and contribute to the design of a more inclusive and multifaceted look. This may provide a hint to why offices inspired by the Knoll look have worked so well as backdrops for discriminatory modes of interaction, as suggested, for instance, by the previously mentioned television series *Mad Men*.

One of the prevailing threads in Florence Knoll's design language clearly derives from the lessons she learnt from Eliel (who, it must be noted, was more loyal to the tenets of total design in theory than in practice). Loja's influence was initially less noticeable, although it remained as an underlying strand that would surface more prominently in the later stages of Knoll's career.

Like each of his parents, Eero Saarinen also forged his own particular connection with Florence Knoll.

> Eero Saarinen suggested that I plan and make (as far as my ability) the furnishings of my dormitory room. I designed an all in one desk top, bookcase, headboard combination and a simple cube table on rollers. In the weaving department, I started a striped carpet, some upholstery and as I progressed in skill, a geometric wall hanging influenced by Loja Saarinen. The metal arm chair in the sketch was previously designed for Kingswood by Eero—it is interesting to reflect the same relation happened at Knoll when Eero designed chairs and I designed what I referred to as the "fill-in" pieces—mostly cabinetry. The Cranbrook experience certainly enhanced my ability to deal with the myriad design problems in the years to come at Knoll.[35] (Plate 5)

He was seven years older than her, and their relationship was close. She included in her collected papers several letters "drawn" by him, which show a playful, warm, and clearly affectionate mood. (Fig. 18) Knoll also stressed on several occasions how much she had learned from Eero. "Because he was my big brother, kind of, he would criticize my work tremendously because he wanted me to do the best. He taught me a lot."[36] When she first got close to the Saarinens, Eero's parents hoped that he and Florence would in the future become a

Opposite, Fig. 17: Cord installation at Knoll Showroom, 601 Madison Avenue, New York, by Florence Knoll/Knoll Planning Unit and Herbert Matter, photograph by Robert Damora, 1948 (Courtesy of Knoll Archives)

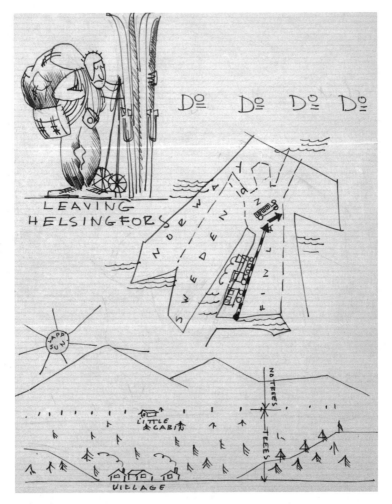

Fig. 18: Letter to Florence Knoll, by Eero Saarinen, 1936 (Florence Knoll Basset papers, Archives of American Art, Smithsonian Institution)

couple, she reported in an interview. As a matter of fact, they did have a romantic link for a short period of time.[37] Knoll said, however, she could have never married him and taken the risk of remaining forever in his shadow.

The two would eventually play important roles in each other's lives—both personally and professionally. It is significant, for example, that Florence Knoll considered that the first iteration of the Knoll look happened in the dormitory room project, which was initiated by Eero. Even more significantly, Eero would become one of the main furniture designers to work for Knoll Associates. He was the author of the Grasshopper Chair (1946), the Womb Chair (1948), and the Pedestal Collection (1957), among many other iconic and commercially very successful furniture pieces. Eero's "designs, which employed modern materials in graceful, organic shapes, helped establish the reputation and identity of Knoll during its formative years."[38] Florence Knoll, in turn, would design several interiors for Eero's buildings. They include the gigantic General Motors Technical Center in Warren, Michigan (1950), Drake University in Des Moines, Iowa (1954), and the thirty-five-floor skyscraper for the Columbia Broadcasting Systems (CBS) in New York (1964), the very last project Florence Knoll designed for Knoll Associates.

> In some ways, you could say Eero and his work as a designer influenced me to pursue the life I did. He was the most partic-ular of all the designers I worked with, always concerned with every little detail and every little form. Eero Saarinen had more imagination and honesty in his work than any designer active during his lifetime. His contributions to the modern era are unmatched by any of his contemporaries.[39]

Those who did not like Eero Saarinen's work classified it as "corporate advertising."[40] An unsupportive critic could, in fact, attribute the same label to Knoll's interiors. There was, clearly, a symbiosis between the production of these two designers, which continued to reflect also in their lives. "His relationship with Florence Schust Knoll remained as close as ever through her widowhood, his affairs, his divorce from Lily [artist Lilian Swann Saarinen (1912–95)], and both of their remarriages."[41] The rapport between Eero and Florence was, it seems, genuine, and their connection was certainly very productive from a professional point of view. There was an underlying assumption, however, that their relationship was established on the understanding that he was a better designer than she was. During the Cranbrook years, Eero took the position of a mentor, more than a friend, to Florence. There were the history lessons at Hvitträsk, where he took the role of a teacher and she, of a student. There was the fact that he studied (and excelled) at the highly prestigious Yale University (he finished the architecture course in three years, rather than the four that were the standard at the time). There were his impressive, intimidating drawing skills (mentioned above). And there was his parents' exceptional admiration and encouragement, which also seems to have made an impact on the professional development of Eero's sister, Pipsan. (Pipsan became a fairly accomplished interior and furniture designer. However, within her family and elsewhere, she never received nearly the same level of recognition as her brother.)

> Perpetuating the gender roles she had been raised with, Loja reminded her daughter through example that she had given up her career for more important duties, namely, to raise her children and support her husband. For Eero, or "Poju" (Sonny), who as a toddler made paper octahedrons and dodecahedrons while pestering draftsmen with questions, she had nothing but praise. To all, she extolled him as a genius destined for a glorious career in the arts. Pipsan, certainly as accomplished as her younger brother in her childhood, never received the same praise.[42]

During Florence Knoll's years at Knoll Associates, while she focused her career on interiors, which had a lower professional ranking than architecture, she also downplayed her own contribution to furniture design. "I was never really

Fig. 19: Examples of "meat and potatoes" furniture, by Florence Knoll, photograph by Martin Helfer, circa 1950s (Courtesy of Knoll Archives)

a furniture designer," she said many times.[43] This statement was partially related to the fact that her furniture work, unlike Eero's, was not "sculptural." This despite of the fact that Knoll's furniture occupied on average half of the pieces on offer in the Knoll catalogs, and that it "filled the offices of Planning Unit projects at a greater rate than any other designer."[44] (Fig. 19)

The assumption that Eero Saarinen was a superior designer to Florence Knoll holds together within the logic of

Fig. 20: Knoll Showroom, Chicago, by Florence Knoll/Knoll Planning Unit, 1953 (Courtesy of Knoll Archives)

the star system, which praises authorship based on a clearly
identifiable signature and relies on work displaying cutting
edge, innovative, original features. If, instead, one considers
factors like longevity or resilience, Florence Knoll's contribution rates higher. Her way of working has proven to endure,
evolve, and spread in prolific directions. It has influenced
design and culture, more generally, in ways that are not
always obvious but that have a strong and lasting impact (as
evidenced, for example, by the influence of her interiors in the
above-mentioned television series). "Practices which are now
commonplace in interior design—such as maintenance man-
uals, three-dimensional presentation models, and furniture
layout plans with fabric swatches attached—originated with
her."[45]

For all her unassuming personality, Knoll was aware of
the extent of her contribution. "The furniture I designed for
mass production had finally sifted into the Sears Roebuck
catalog. I think that speaks for the practicality of the design."[46]
Only, as far as her creative talent and abilities were concerned,
she would not dare claim a similar position to Eero and to
other of her male colleagues.

In many of the Knoll Associates interiors, Florence Knoll
repeated the formula she had first experimented with in her
dormitory scheme under Eero's encouragement. This formula included highlighting primary colors against the more
discrete hues of whites, beiges, and blacks. It also invariably
incorporates the presence of plants, the warming effect of
textiles and artworks, and the subdued addition of Knoll's
"meat and potatoes" furniture against the visual dominance
of the more "sculptural" work of other designers. In some
cases, perhaps under a more direct influence of Eero's design
approach, Knoll herself created some "sculptural" features to
help shape her interiors. This can be noticed, for instance, in
her work for several Knoll showrooms: in the bold triangular

Fig. 21: Knoll Showroom, Miami, by Florence Knoll/Knoll Planning Unit, 1959 (Courtesy of Knoll Archives)

ceiling planks in Milan; in the more subtle origami-shaped forms in Chicago; and in the vaulted spaces in Los Angeles and Miami. (Plate 8, Figs. 20-21)

If Florence Knoll and Eero Saarinen shared the talent to create memorable schemes well suited to the corporate environment, they seem to have achieved this through different means. His work instigated surprise, presenting, for each different brief, a bold, assertive, and brand-new form. Hers, instead, tended to concentrate the elements of surprise on smaller details—sculptural chairs in most cases, but also other features, as outlined above. These details, on the whole, articulated a language that would, with time, feel familiar as a consequence of repetition. Because Knoll's focus was on language more than on the surprise factor of each separate scheme, she succeeded in creating an identity that became associated with a typology—the modern office—rather than with a person. In that, her legacy is fundamentally different from Eero's.

The influence the Saarinens had on Florence Knoll's career went beyond the special relationships she developed with Eero, Loja, and Eliel.[47] Through them, not only did she have the opportunity to meet fellow students from Cranbrook—some of whom would eventually become notorious professionals in the creative fields—she was also introduced to a wide social and professional network, which included some of the best known architects and artists of the time.

> After graduation from Kingswood in 1934, Eliel Saarinen suggested that I spend some time at the [Cranbrook] academy before attending an accredited architectural school. This offered a great opportunity to live and work in an atmosphere of creativity and serious work with great artists like the Saarinens and Carl Milles [1875-1955] and advanced students. It also provided me with time to concentrate on design.[48] (Fig. 22)

Fig. 22: Florence Knoll and Swedish sculptor Carl Milles (Courtesy of Cranbrook Archives, Cranbrook Center for Collections and Research)

Following her period at the Cranbrook Academy of Art, in 1935, Knoll started her formal training at the Columbia University School of Architecture, as a student in the Town Planning program. There, she briefly met Le Corbusier (1887–1965).[49] She did not, however, return to Columbia in the

autumn of 1936, but underwent surgery in Michigan. When
she recovered she enrolled again in the architecture course at
Cranbrook. It was during this period that Knoll met people
like Marianne Strengell (1909–98), an accomplished textile
designer and educator who would supply patterns to Knoll
Textiles in the late 1940s; and Harry Bertoia, future creator
of a Knoll classic: the Diamond Chair. Bertoia remembers his
first encounter with Knoll as "brief," but "kind of marvelous":
"I was a student, and since the student body was perhaps
thirty-five at that time, naturally you met everyone. When I
entered the home of Eliel and Loja Saarinen, she was reclin-
ing on a big beautiful Saarinen-designed sofa."[50]

While spending the summer of 1937 with the Saarinens
in Finland, Florence Knoll met Alvar Aalto (1898–1976), and
he then advised her to enroll at the Architectural Association
in London. Starting in the winter of the same year, Knoll
spent two years at the AA, where she encountered a lively
student community and an engaged, forward-thinking educational culture. From the AA, Knoll wrote to her former tutor
Rachel DeWolfe Raseman, saying that her main goal while
at the school was to "learn about construction."[51] For this, she
would have found the support of professionals like Ove Arup
(1895–1988, lecturer in Advanced Design in Concrete Construction) and Maxwell Fry (1899–1987, guest critic). It was
also during her AA years that Knoll first experimented with
the suiting fabrics she would later source for the upholstering of Knoll furniture in the mid 1940s. "She later recalled
that the idea of using this type of fabric originated in a 'very
handsome Scottish linen of heavy weight' which she had
used in her student days at the Architectural Association in
London."[52]

With the eruption of World War II in 1939, Knoll was
forced to return to the US. Before continuing her training, she
interned at the office of Marcel Breuer and Walter Gropius

in Cambridge, Massachusetts. Her main contribution in the office was toward one of their largest and most important residential projects, the Frank House in Pittsburgh, where she is thought to have designed the children's rooms. While working for Breuer and Gropius, Knoll also had contact, probably for the first time, with the work of textile designer Anni Albers (1899–1994), another important future contributor at Knoll Associates, who was in charge of designing furnishings for Breuer and Gropius's scheme.

In 1940, Knoll enrolled at the Armour Institute in Chicago (which became the Illinois Institute of Technology [IIT] that same year). She studied there under Mies van der Rohe, who, she said, "had a profound effect on my design approach and the clarification of design."[53] From Mies, Knoll learned to appreciate the "creativity of form, the honesty of materials, the creative elevation of industrial production."[54] Noticeably, she also managed to strike a personal relationship with the celebrated German architect and future collaborator. "I lived very close to the hotel where Mies lived and frequently when I would walk home from the school in the evening, I would stop for coffee on the way and talk to Mies. It was a great bonus."[55] Florence Knoll graduated from IIT in 1941 with a bachelor of science degree in architecture.

The influence Mies's work had on Florence Knoll's is palpable. She had established the basic ingredients that would constitute the Knoll look in her Cranbrook dormitory project, yet it was through engaging with Mies's work that Knoll would refine her design language. Mies's architecture was remarkable in its combination of technical precision and artistic intention. This formula suited the Knoll brief particularly well. The technical aspect lent to the design a sense of robustness and reliability—necessary to boost the image of the corporations and institutions that housed it—while the artistic touch made each work feel new and exciting—another great

Fig. 23: Knoll Showroom, San Francisco, by Florence Knoll/Knoll Planning Unit, 1954 (Courtesy of Knoll Archives)

marketing tool for Florence Knoll's future company. Mies
van der Rohe was, unlike Eero Saarinen, a great believer in
the power of repetition in design. "Architecture is a language
having the discipline of a grammar," he wrote. "Language can
be used for normal day-to-day purposes as a prose. And if you
are very good you can be a poet."[56] Mies acknowledged the
necessity of learning how to calibrate design, from "prose" to
"poetry," so different projects could meet considerably different demands while still somehow belonging together. This,
again, would prove to be a handy tool for Florence Knoll, given
that she was engaged with the creation of a look that had to be
both adaptable and identifiable at the same time. "The mission
of the Knoll Planning Unit was to create the visual language
of the modern office interior and to make it inhabitable," as
she defined.[57]

"Advancing technology provided the builder with new
materials and more efficient methods which were often in
glaring contrast to our traditional conception of architecture,"
Mies wrote.[58] Modernist architects felt it was their mission
to respond to these new technologies, exploring how the
constructional procedures they entailed could generate new
design solutions. Le Corbusier and Eero Saarinen, for example, focused their design research mainly on the possibilities
of reinforced concrete. Mies, conversely, opted for steel. Steel
was, as it happens, also a very suitable material for the interior work Florence Knoll would develop. The dry method of
building with metal allowed for fast systems of assembly that
could produce radical transformations in interior settings
with—compared to concrete construction techniques—
minimal hassle. As previously discussed with regard to the
Knoll Showroom at 601 Madison Avenue, New York, Knoll
made great use of metal structures to alter the ambience
and spatial dynamic of her designs. One notable example
was the Knoll Showroom in San Francisco (1954), where she

transformed a dull, shoebox-shaped warehouse into a rather agreeable and humane two-story interior setting through the introduction of simple metal cages. (Fig. 23)

Finding design solutions based on technological procedures meant—in the cases of modernist architects like Eero Saarinen, Le Corbusier, and Mies van der Rohe—that materials and structure would now play a role that was not only pragmatic but also symbolic: they would take the part that was previously assigned to ornament. Steel structure, for Mies, "while not in itself architecture," could "be a means of architecture."[59] The structure, for Mies, changed from playing a supportive role in the building to carrying its very cultural significance. "I want a structural architecture, because I believe that that is the only way by which we can have a communion with the essentials of our civilization," he argued.[60]

Architects started to rely on an understanding of design as the search for "an artistic solution for an otherwise purely utilitarian problem."[61] These "utilitarian problems" ranged from technological issues, as discussed above, to programmatic ones, including exercises required to give shape to relatively new typologies, such as the factory and the office.[62] While Mies focused a great part of his creative energy on finding an "artistic solution" to the problem of the steel structure, Florence Knoll concentrated hers on doing the same for the corporate office.

The first offices of the late nineteenth and early twentieth centuries approached program in a predominantly pragmatic fashion. They were designed in a way that people, as well as paperwork, would flow as quickly and smoothly as possible in order to maximize efficiency. "The seconds required to walk the 50 feet for a drink at the fountain was time not spent pressing buttons, recording dictation, or filing documents; those precious lost seconds were considered to be the consequence of faulty architectural planning."[63] The "scientific

Fig. 24: Florence Knoll's version of a "sanitary desk," circa 1950s
(Courtesy of Knoll Archives)

Fig. 25: Detail of Florence Knoll's version of a "sanitary desk," circa 1950s (Courtesy of Knoll Archives)

office manager," a new type of professional, was in charge of securing maximum performance in terms of the office interior as well as its furniture design.

As to the design of the desk, a "sanitary" one, lifted on slender legs, was strongly preferred over the older designs; traditional bureaus that descended all the way to the floor were believed to harbour dust or dirt that can accumulate without being seen. Even more problematic were the traditional patent-cabinet or roll-top desks. Those desks had been designed for the clerks of the pre-corporate era—enclosed, self-sufficient work-stations filled with numerous cubbies, enclosures, slots, and drawers to contain his hand-copied papers and ledger books. In the corporate Taylorist age, however, these enclosed desks began to look like vaults, dangerous traps into which important papers might fall, slipping out of the paperwork channel and becoming lost and abandoned. The sanitary desk—with its clean, flat surface on which all vital papers remained visible—afforded no sanctuaries into which renegade papers might slip.[64] (Figs. 24, 25)

The elements of the modern office had already been invented when Florence Knoll started her professional career. Modeled on the typology of the factory, these spaces favored efficiency over comfort, creating a culture ruled by authority that, some claimed, rendered workers psychologically vulnerable, "susceptible to propaganda," and prone to "soothe the egos of those in power."[65]

> The pre-war office with its repeating rows of identical desks and chairs became emblematic of this standardised, conformist, corporate culture. The unstylised, uniform furniture and layout supported the belief that corporate culture required individuals to sacrifice their identities in order to do well.[66]

Under Florence Knoll, the character of the office changed. In the same way that Mies, through his artistic skills, had turned the steel structure, in principle dull and monotonous, into an iconic design feature, Knoll transformed the equally boring

Fig. 26: Knoll Showroom, Chicago, by Florence Knoll/Knoll Planning Unit, photograph by Yuichi Idaka, 1953 (Florence Knoll Basset papers, Archives of American Art, Smithsonian Institution)

and standardized modern office into an image that was eventually considered to be cool and sexy.

> Prior to the existence of the Knoll Planning Unit, what a visitor to a major corporation might have seen was a modestly practical and totally uninspired interior, most often characterized by stereotypical steel desks topped with green linoleum. It was a time when no thought was given to serious planning of furniture. Planning work was usually done by a purchasing agent who picked up a catalog and just ordered so many desks. The top executive sometimes had an interior decorator or the building architect to do heavy walnut paneling. That was about it.[67]

"Everything was so bad," Florence Knoll summed up, "it was very easy to improve it."[68]

The Knoll showrooms were important for Florence Knoll to demonstrate her vision for the modern interior. She innovated on this front as well, averting the warehouse style that was the standard for showrooms at the time—and that showed "just a whole lot of furniture in rows"—in favor of creating settings with a strong sense of atmosphere.[69] Knoll showrooms would become the main selling points of the Knoll look, and Florence Knoll considered them to be "her proudest accomplishments."[70] (Fig. 26)

> Since the showrooms were designed specifically to win clients over to contemporary design, Knoll understood that they could not just be a collection of rooms, even nicely designed, that incorporated the expected features of a good office—rather, in order to convey a fantasy which would affect their clients and leave an impression in their minds, Knoll often built spaces that were more dramatic than the interiors of typical offices. Indeed, despite the company's specialisation in office interiors,

most of Knoll showrooms displayed living-room and lounge arrangements rather than office models.[71]

Florence Knoll's interiors glamorized the space of the office and, consequentially, they glamorized work, promoting it not as a means to an end, but as an end in itself. As demonstrated in the interiors and lifestyle of the *Mad Men* television series, the Knoll look combined the image of efficiency that was required from a working space with the excitement and drama that is usually linked to leisure and entertainment, adding to the mix a cozy and intimate experience typically associated with the domestic.[72] It was as if the office as a space, and work as an activity, now contained everything that a human being needed in order to feel happy and ful-filled. In this sense, the Knoll look promoted the culture that is today associated with companies like Google and Facebook, and with coworking spaces like WeWork and NeueHouse.

From Mies, Knoll learned to refine and glamorize the realm of the utilitarian. While this enabled her to create highly sophisticated and seductive working spaces, it also con-tributed to the endorsement of an alienating working culture, created for the good of corporations and not of individuals: "The blurring of spatial boundaries between work and non-work encourages employees to identify more closely with organizations, and gets them to channel a larger aspect of their lives and energies—their relationships, affects, and cre-ativity—for the purposes of corporate gain."[73] Furthermore, as previously suggested, the fact that this culture originated in the early- to mid-twentieth century, a period where the sphere of work was still largely dominated by men, implies that the environments designed for office work reproduce similarly male-dominated conditions. In Florence Knoll's time,

[t]he business professionals all followed the example of doctors, lawyers, and ministers, by attempting, with varying degrees of success, to exclude women from their ranks. As far as early business professionals were concerned, women and feminine influence had to be excluded from the managerial ethos or its masculine purity would be threatened.[74]

The Knoll look worked in favor of an exploitative culture that remains to this day ubiquitous. There were, notwithstanding, considerable variations to the language Florence Knoll created for the modern working interior, each having substantial implications to the way in which it impacted its activities and users. The next chapter will dive deeper into the Knoll look, to discuss its variations and their significance.

NOTES

1. "Biographical Material," 102.

2. Warren, "Woman Who Led Office."

3. "Biographical Material," 102.

4. "Biographical Material," 9.

5. Throughout her life, Florence Knoll mentioned Raseman's (whose name changed to Rachel Elizabeth DeWolfe Black after she remarried in 1950) important influence on her career. "Rachel was a wonderful role model," she said. "It was so rare then for a woman to be an architect, and to have one as one's high school teacher and mentor was extraordinary." (Pat Kirkham and Lynne Walker, "Women Designers in the USA, 1900–2000: Diversity and Difference," in Pat Kirkham, ed., *Women Designers in the USA, 1900–2000* [New Haven: Yale University Press, 2000], 406n55). It is, however, hard to know precisely what influence she had on Knoll's professional development, as not much is known about her views and position on design. Raseman was one of only two hundred women then practicing architecture in the US. She went to Cranbrook to accompany her husband Richard P. Raseman, also an architect, who worked as executive secretary and vice president of the Cranbrook Academy of Art from 1932 until 1943. After leaving Cranbrook in 1942, Raseman became architect-in-residence with Frank Lloyd Wright in Taliesin, Arizona. She then moved to Los Angeles, where she started an interior design business called California Contempora. In 1950, Raseman moved to New Hope and joined her second husband in his business of selling Christmas trees that they grew on their farm. See Amy L. Arnold and Jessica L. Puff, "The Knoll Look: Florence Schust Knoll Bassett and the Reinvention of the Modern Interior," in Amy L. Arnold and Brian D. Conway, eds., *Michigan Modern: Design That Shaped America* (Layton, Utah: Gibbs Smith, 2016), 190; "Richard P. Raseman Papers, 1934–1956," Cranbrook, accessed March 30, 2019, http://www.cranbrook.edu/sites/default/files/ftpimages/120/misc/misc_54585.pdf; and "Rachel DeWolfe Black," Bucks County Artist Database, accessed June 25, 2020, https://bucksco.michenerartmuseum.org/artists/rachel-de-wolfe-black.

6. "Biographical Material," 9.

7. Ibid.

8. Mark Coir, "The Cranbrook Factor," in Eeva-Liisa Pelkonen and Donald Albrecht, *Eero Saarinen: Shaping the Future* (New Haven and London: Yale University Press, 2006), 32, and Paul Goldberger, "The Cranbrook Vision: The Metropolitan Museum Commemorates an American Giant among Schools of Design," *New York Times Magazine*, April 8, 1984, 49–55.

9. Ibid.

10. Ibid.

11. "Biographical Material," 102.

12. "Subject Files". Florence Knoll Bassett Papers, Archives of American Art, Smithsonian Institution (Series 5, folder 2, 32).

13. Florence Knoll Bassett Papers, Archives of American Art, Smithsonian Institution. Knoll's family included some affluent and successful members, such as her cousins Edward Heinemann, an aviation engineer who designed military planes for Douglas Aircraft; Howard Kehrl, a research engineer and vice chairman of General Motors; and George Housner, a pioneer in earthquake engineering. See Arnold and Puff, "Knoll Look," 190.

14. "Biographical Material," 105.

15. History, About, Cranbrook Academy of Art, accessed April 18, 2018, https://cranbrookart.edu/about/history/.

16. Rosalind P. Blakesley, *The Arts and Crafts Movement* (London: Phaidon, 2006), 7.

17. See Albert Christ-Janer, *Eliel Saarinen* (Chicago: University of Chicago Press, 1948), 9.

18. Ibid., 12. Importantly, in the early twentieth century, the realm of ornamentation was closely associated with the manifestation of femininity as well as to work produced by women. See Rae Beth Gordon, *Ornament, Fantasy, and Desire in Nineteenth-Century French Literature* (Princeton: Princeton University Press, 1992) and Rozsika Parker, *The Subversive Stitch: Embroidery and the Making of the Feminine* (London: I.B. Tauris, 2010).

19. Christ-Janer, *Eliel Saarinen*, 11.

20. Ibid., 12.

21. Larrabee and Vignelli, *Knoll Design*, 57.

22. Lutz, *Knoll*, 29.

23. Warren, "Woman Who Led Office."

24. Walter Benjamin, *The Arcades Project*, trans. Howard Eiland (Cambridge, MA: Harvard University Press, 1999), 9.

25. Ibid.

26. *Cambridge Dictionary Online*, s.v. "phantasmagoria," accessed September 18, 2019, https://dictionary.cambridge.org/dictionary/english/phantasmagoria.

27. "Drawings, Sketches and Designs," Florence Knoll Bassett Papers, Archives of American Art, Smithsonian Institution (Series 3, folder 3, 11).

28. "Subject Files," Folder 2, 44.

29. "Subject Files," Folder 20, 3.

30. Charles Baudelaire, "The Painter of Modern Life," in *The Painter of Modern Life and Other Essays*, trans. and ed. Jonathan Mayne (London: Phaidon, 1964), 33.

31. Paul Makovsky, "Knoll before Knoll Textiles," in Martin, *Knoll Textiles*, 88–89.

32. Christopher Breward, *The Hidden Consumer: Masculinity, Fashion and City Life 1860–1914* (Manchester: Manchester University Press, 1999), 2.

33. "Subject Files," Folder 10, 2.

34. There are numerous examples of how interior decorators working in the first half of the twentieth century would play with non-Western features in a less contrived manner. See for example Penny Sparke, *Elsie de Wolfe: The Birth of Modern Interior Decoration* (New York: Acanthus, 2005).

35. "Biographical Material," 12.

36. Lutz, *Knoll*, 43.

37. See Coir, "Cranbrook Factor."

38. See "Eero Saarinen," Our Designers, Discover Knoll, Knoll, accessed August 24, 2019, https://www.knoll.com/designer/Eero-Saarinen.

39. Florence Schust Knoll Bassett, "Preface," in Brian Lutz, *Eero Saarinen: Furniture for Everyman* (New York: Pointed Leaf Press, 2012), 6.

40. Vincent Scully, "Reframing Saarinen," in Pelkonen and Albrecht, *Eero Saarinen*, 13.

41. Coir, "Cranbrook Factor," 41.

42. Ibid., 30–31.

43. Joseph Giovannini, "Florence Knoll: Form, Not Fashion," *New York Times*, April 7, 1983, unnumbered.

44. Tigerman, "Not a Decorator," 70.

45. Sylvia Katz and Jeremy Myerson, "First Lady of the Modern Office," *World Architecture UK* (1990), 78.

46. Jo Werne, "She Shaped Knoll into a Major Force in Design," *Miami Herald*, October 25, 1981, unnumbered.

47. It is in some ways intriguing that Florence Knoll did not develop a significant relationship with Pipsan Saarinen (later Pipsan Saarinen Swanson), given that they shared the same profession. Pipsan was twelve years older than Florence. She taught at the Cranbrook Academy of Art from the early 1930s until 1935, so she would have been around when Knoll was a student. Pipsan practiced interiors in the company her husband Robert Swanson (1900–1981) founded in Detroit in 1933, Swanson Associates (she became a partner of the company in 1944). They had been married since 1926. Robert Swanson was a close friend of Henry Booth (who had introduced the Saarinens to his parents, the founders of the Cranbrook Educational Community) and worked with him, Eliel and Eero Saarinen before founding Swanson Associates. In 1950, Pipsan and Robert Swanson won a prestigious furniture award in the inaugural event of the *Good Design* exhibition, co-sponsored by the Musem of Modern Art (MoMA) in New York. By this time, Florence Knoll was already a partner of Knoll Associates and she would very likely have been aware of the work the Swansons were doing. She does not, however, mention it in her papers or elsewhere. It is also striking to notice that in the many letters Loja Saarinen sent to Florence Knoll, there is plenty of reference to Eero and Eliel, but not to Pipsan. See "Pipsan: the Lesser-known (but no less Impressive!) Saarinen Sibling," Cranbrook Art Museum, accessed June 26, 2020, https://cranbrookartmuseum.org/2014/03/31/pipsan-the-lesser-known-but-no-less-impressive-saarinen-sibling/; "J. Robert F. Swanson and Pipsan Saarinen Swanson," Cranbrook Archives, accessed June 26, 2020, https://www.cranbrook.edu/sites/default/files/ftpimages/120/misc/misc_35148.pdf; "Letters," Florence Knoll Bassett Papers, Archives of American Art, Smithsonian Institution (Series 6).

48. "Biographical Material," 12.

49. See Paul Makovsky, "Total Design: How Florence Knoll Revolutionised Design and the Modern Interior," paper presented at AA XX 100: AA Women and Architecture in Context 1917–2017, Architectural Association, London, on November 3, 2017.

50. "Celebrating 100 Years of Florence Knoll," Knoll, accessed April 19, 2018, https://www.knoll.com/story/shop/fkb-100.

51. Makovsky, "Total Design."

52. Makovsky, "Knoll before Knoll Textiles," 89.

53. "Biographical Material," 10.

54. Lutz, *Knoll*, 12.

55. Ibid., 26.

56. Kenneth Frampton, "The Unknown Mies van der Rohe," in David Spaeth, *Mies van der Rohe* (New York: Rizzoli, 1985), 8.

57. Arnold and Puff, "Knoll Look," 192.

58. Frampton, "Unknown Mies," 7.

59. Ludwig Hilberseimer, *Mies van der Rohe* (Chicago: Paul Theobald, 1956), 12.

60. Spaeth, *Mies van der Rohe*, 16.

61. Amy L. Arnold, "Pure Design: The Modern Legacy of Emil Lorch and the Architecture Program at the University of Michigan," in Arnold and Conway, *Michigan Modern*, 73.

62. For an understanding of the emerging typology of the office, see Ronn M. Daniel, "Taylorizing the Modern Interior," in Jo Ann Asher Thompson and Nancy H. Blossom, eds., *The Handbook of Interior Design* (Chichester, UK: John Wiley & Sons, 2015), 58–69.

63. Ibid., 62.

64. Ibid., 63.

65. Renyi Hong, "Office Interiors and the Fantasy of Information Work," in *Triple C: Communication, Capitalism & Critique* 15, no. 2 (2017): 540.

66. Ibid.

67. Lutz, Knoll, 29.

68. Ibid.

69. Ibid., 35. The Hermann Miller furniture company started redesigning showrooms "as vignettes" even before the Knolls, launching its first such showroom in Chicago in 1939. These showrooms were initially intended for the trade only, meaning only for architects and interior designers, however those professionals often brought their clients with them to see particular products. John R. Berry, *Hermann Miller: Classic Furniture and System Designs for the Working Environment* (London: Thames & Hudson, 2004), 69. Knoll's modern showrooms were so different from what the public was used to that sometimes clients did not realize their purpose. Knoll collaborator Yves Vidal recalled amusingly that when the company first opened its showroom in Paris in the 1950s, showing furniture "grouped together like an office or living room, with flowers and plants," most of the visitors thought the owners were florists. Larrabee and Vignelli, *Knoll Design*, 195.

70. Lutz, *Knoll*, 38.

71. Hong, "Office Interiors," 547 (emphasis mine).

72. Offices had been modelled after domestic spaces—more specifically, after masculine domestic spaces—since the late nineteenth century. See Angel Kwolek-Folland, "The Gendered Environment of the Corporate Workplace, 1880–1930," in Katharine Martinez and Kenneth L. Ames, eds., *The Material Culture of Gender, The Gender of Material Culture* (Winterthur, DE: Henry Francis du Pont Winterthur Museum, 1997), 157–80.

73. Hong, "Office Interiors," 546.

74. Sharon Hartman Strom, *Beyond the Typewriter: Gender, Class, and the Origins of Modern American Office Work, 1900–1930* (Chicago: University of Chicago Press, 1992), 4–5.

CHAPTER TWO: THE KNOLLS AND THE KNOLL LOOK

Hans Knoll, who, in the mid 1940s, became Florence Knoll's partner in business and in life, had been born into the furniture business.

> I think he was slightly in competition with his family, because the Knoll family, in Germany, they were all furniture manufacturers, and, particularly, his father was, and I think he wanted to better them all.[1]

Hans's grandfather, Wilhelm Knoll (1839–1907), had started his trade in Stuttgart in 1865. He first sold leather, then specialized in quality upholstery and in a self-produced seating line. His business was so successful that it was appointed as a "supplier to the Court" of the Württemberg monarchy.[2] In 1907, Wilhelm's sons Walter (1876–1971) and Wilhelm II (1878–1954) took over the family company, by then named Ledersitzmöbelfabrik (Leather Seating Factory) Wilhelm Knoll, with a view to expand and innovate. The general climate was, at this stage, very different from that when Hans Knoll's grandfather had started, with furniture production becoming increasingly more attuned with industrial development and the demands of the mass market.

The year 1907 was significant for a broader reason, for it was this year that the Deutscher Werkbund was formed in Munich, Germany. The Werkbund, an organization of the leading Figs. in German arts and architecture, created a manifesto that prescribed a union of "art, industry and artisanship." The machine age had arrived, and it was a modernist decision to utilize mass production to serve the growing class of working consumers. Patronage of the applied arts of the Craft era had long been the exclusive province of the privileged class; modernists believed mass consumption could only be enabled by mass production. The Werkbund believed, further, that the introduction of art to the equation would elevate the quality of industrial production.[3]

Even though some of the members of the Deutscher Werkbund association were against industrial standardization, it was their unanimous view that, whatever direction the applied arts industry was to take, it was to engage artists and designers much more actively than it had done in the past. It was also their common opinion that modern products were to target wider audiences. From 1919 the Bauhaus endorsed these principles even more assertively, and this must have somehow filtered into the Knoll family's DNA, for it would define the very ethos guiding the company that Hans and Florence Knoll would run two decades later.

Both Hans Knoll's father, Walter, and his uncle Wilhelm II were modernist enthusiasts. They believed that the new tendencies in architecture demanded a new vision for interiors, favoring "volume over mass, and...decrying all decoration."[4] In the 1920s Hans's uncle Wilhelm II developed the celebrated Antimott Furniture Series, combining wooden frames with elastic strapping to achieve a slimmer, more comfortable and supportive structure for chairs and sofas than contemporary models. The Antimott was so in line with the modernist principles that it was chosen to furnish Zeppelins (an adapted version with aluminum frames was developed for this purpose).[5] The series achieved a considerable reputation, remaining a bestseller for the Wilhelm Knoll Company for many years.

By 1925, Hans's father had split from the family business and founded his own furniture company, Walter Knoll & Co.:

> From the beginning Walter Knoll centered his company's development on the rationalist design ethos of modernism. He developed relationships with Ludwig Mies van der Rohe and Walter Gropius, among others, and supplied upholstered furniture for modernist housing built for the Deutscher Werkbund's 1927 Stuttgart Weissenhof Estate exhibition, the first public exhibition of the architecture and furniture of the Modern Movement.[6]

A year later, in 1928, Walter Knoll & Co. got a patent for a web-steel springing seating system, the Prodomo, which, like the Antimott, allowed for lighter upholstery to be used on chairs, sofas, and lounge chairs. The Prodomo Series (1925–1929) famously employed colored fabrics instead of leather, and, historically, it gained the classification of the first modernist upholstered furniture.[7] Its chairs were also adapted for use in an aircraft, the Do X.[8]

Walter Knoll's company was very successful during the 1930s. It was, however, forced into war production during World War II. Its factory was bombed in 1942 and remained inactive until 1945.[9] By this time, Walter Knoll's son Hans was already consolidating his own company in the US, and in its early days he represented furniture from his father's company.[10]

Following the steps of his grandfather, Hans Knoll started his career in the textile industry. He moved to London in 1933, escaping the difficult political conditions in Germany with the rise of National Socialism, and also his own family situation.

"Hans was not able to work with my father," said his brother
Robert. "He was always a problem."[11] Hans Knoll's first job in
London was for the British brand of an American company
named Jantzen Knitting Mills—a manufacturer of knitted
clothing products. Like the businesses run by the Knoll
brothers Walter and Wilhelm II, the company had a progressive outlook. It promoted new materials such as Lastex
(a rubber-core yarn) and rayon. This first experience in the
textile business certainly influenced Hans Knoll later in life,
helping him define the orientation of his own Knoll Textiles
division in the late 1940s. Hans's second job in London was
working for a friend of his father, the Russian-born architect
Serge Chermayeff (1900–96).[12] Chermayeff had in 1932 started
a furniture and interiors company named Plan Ltd. It specialized in modernist items such as tubular steel furniture,
hand-knotted rugs, and lighting produced in UK factories
under license to foreign manufacturers. Plan was considered
to be "one of the more significant modernist experiments
in the manufacture and retail of contemporary furniture and
furnishings in Britain during the interwar years."[13] Walter
Knoll & Co. was one of its main suppliers, alongside Scottish
textile manufacturers Donald Brothers, which years later provided patterns for Knoll Associates. Plan was, however, badly
affected by the tensions leading to World War II, and by 1938
it had been dissolved.

Likely influenced by the instability provoked by the war,
Hans Knoll relocated to the US in 1937. His initial plan was
to stay for one year only, but he must have changed his mind
quickly, as by early 1939 he was already married to a woman
from Long Island named Barbara Southwick. In 1938, Hans
started working as a salesman for George Ditmar, a furniture
retailer and wholesaler with a showroom on Madison Avenue.
Two years later, he incorporated himself as Hans G. Knoll
Furniture Company, selling some lines from Walter Knoll &

Co., together with other American products. "He had one good chair that he brought over from Germany," Florence Knoll remembered. "It was an excellent design. It had a marvelous spring system which has never quite been equaled."[14] One of Hans's company's first successful deals was with the Mueller Furniture Company of Grand Rapids, a large American manufacturer based in Florence's native Michigan.[15] He was as well, for a short period in 1941, a wholesale sales representative for Artek, the company that produced, distributed, and promoted Alvar Aalto's furniture. Following the model of Serge Chermayeff's Plan in London, Hans Knoll took interior design commissions whenever these became available. Thanks to these commissions, two years later he met and then started to collaborate with his future partner Florence Knoll.

Hans Knoll's business gained new focus when he hired Danish designer Jens Risom (1916–2016) in 1941. Risom had emigrated from Copenhagen in 1939, where he had graduated in architecture and furniture design and worked in retail and interiors. He had since been designing textiles and furniture for a small but respected New York dealer called Dan Cooper. Risom's pieces attracted the attention of some modernist devotees when they were shown at the exhibition *House of Ideas*, curated by architect Edward Durrell Stone (1902–78) at the Rockefeller Center in 1940. His meeting with Hans Knoll soon after this event was providential. "Basically, Hans Knoll and I spent the next year looking for each other without knowing it," he wrote.[16]

> Hans Knoll found customers and projects and Risom designed the interiors, the furnishings, and furniture. Together Knoll and Risom brought a fresh new style to the interiors of offices and homes. The customers Hans Knoll found—business, architect or celebrity—had one thing in common: a preference for the emergent modernist style put forward by these young Europeans.[17]

In their quest to convert the American market to the modernist taste, Knoll and Risom, together with their wives, embarked on a tour of the US in the summer of 1941. They stopped in Tennessee, where they had to oversee a large residential contract, and also visited Dallas, Los Angeles, San Francisco, and Chicago, among other cities. During their trip, the duo approached leading architects and designers and visited contemporary furniture stores in order to "feel" the market. They had been tipped with a list of key contacts by the influential publisher and editor of *Architectural Forum*, Howard Myers (1894–1947), whose wife, Louise (1896–1968), had been hired by Hans Knoll as an office manager.

> One of Hans Knoll's closest contacts in New York at the time was Howard Myers. Myers liked Knoll and he liked what Knoll was trying to do. Knoll, cleverly, hired Myer's wife to manage his office, and the courtesy and respect between Myers and Knoll provided a strong link for Knoll to the American architectural community.[18]

By the end of their tour, Knoll and Risom were optimistic. "We were convinced that if we did things right, did it well, and fast enough, we would succeed."[19] The main outcome of their joint "market research" was the first Knoll collection, compiled in a catalog where most of the furniture had been designed, exclusively for Knoll, by Risom. The catalog also included one page featuring a textile by an established designer named Frances Breese Miller (1893–1985) and some other, less remarkable, pieces of furniture.[20] In line with the Deutscher Werkbund and Bauhaus philosophies, Hans G. Knoll Furniture Company used designer names as a means to add value to its products and paid the designers royalties for their work.

It was not, however, until they created their second collection that Hans Knoll and Jens Risom managed to nail a more distinctive character for the products of the Hans G. Knoll Furniture Company. Ironically, this was achieved thanks to the shortages of the war years. As it was virtually impossible to get hold of upholstery textiles or, in fact, of any other upholstery material in the early 1940s, Risom was forced to think of an alternative. The result was the elegant 650 Line, which replaced traditional upholstery with an interlaced cotton webbing, using, in its early versions, defective parachute straps that did not meet government specifications to serve the war industry.

> The 650 Line was intended for project use during wartime. We could only use non-critical materials for production such as parachute straps that had been rejected by the military. We had to depend on small workshops or small factories that didn't qualify for war production. Hans was quite good at this; he knew where every place was that was still making furniture.[21]

Although the solution was not exactly original (straps had been used for upholstery by earlier twentieth-century Scandinavian designers), it was fresh enough to excite the American consumer—not least because it bore the soft Scandinavian touch that provided a smooth transition from traditional styles to the new modernist taste. The 650 Chair became the first Knoll classic and is produced to this day, now under the name of Risom Chair. (Fig. 1)

Knoll and Risom managed to secure some remarkable commissions in the early 1940s. Johnson & Johnson and General Motors were, for instance, in their 1941 list of clients. These were, however, relatively small jobs, not nearly as impactful as the work the company would develop later under the guidance and leadership of Florence Knoll.

Fig. 1: 650 Chair (Risom Chair), by Jens Risom, 1943 (Florence Knoll Basset papers, Archives of American Art, Smithsonian Institution)

After graduating from IIT in 1941, Florence Knoll moved to New York, where she freelanced for several architects. They included the Bauhaus polymath Herbert Bayer (1900–85), the French-born industrial designer Raymond Loewy (1893–1986), and the Harvard-educated Richard Marsh Bennett (1907–96). Knoll also moonlighted for Harrison & Abramovitz—the partnership of Wallace K. Harrison (1895–1981), Jacques-André Fouilhoux (1879–1945), and Max Abramovitz (1908–2004)—the architects who became known for prestigious projects such as the UN Headquarters in New York (1952), the original CIA Headquarters in Langley, Virginia (1961), and New York's Lincoln Center for the Performing Arts (1962–66).[22] These architects later gave Knoll Associates some of its first important commissions. While working for Harrison & Abramovitz, Florence met Hans Knoll.

He needed help developing interior commissions he had just
secured, so they started collaborating. The first project in
which they worked together was the office of the US Secretary of War, Henry L. Stimson, in the recently built Pentagon
(1941). The design did not yet display the aesthetic qualities
of the future Knoll look. However, its strategy and program
as an office-integrated interior pointed toward what Knoll
Associates would become famous for a few years later.

Hans Knoll, whom Florence Knoll described as "the
great empire builder," had an impulsive character.[23] He used
to make promises before having the means to deliver them,
and, eventually, things could go wrong. Thanks to one of
Hans's ill-judged decisions, Florence found the opportunity to
become his business partner. In 1944, Hans made a deal with
Bloomingdale's, a leading New York department store, to sell
his furniture. The agreement resulted in a loss of $50,000
(roughly $700,000 in 2019), which Florence covered using
her inheritance fund. As a result, she became a co-owner of
Hans G. Knoll Furniture Company. A few months later she
started to work as its design director, and in 1946 the business
changed its name to Knoll Associates.[24] Florence Knoll had,
from the outset, a bolder design vision than the duo Hans
Knoll and Jens Risom. "I felt they were too romantic," she
said. Even though she had specified furniture designed by
Risom for some of the early interiors she designed for Hans
Knoll, she actually felt they "didn't quite fit in with contemporary architecture."[25] Conveniently, in 1943, Risom had to leave
the company to join the army. When he returned in 1945 he
found a completely different organization from the one he had
left and decided to quit an- start his own business.

The basic structure of the future Knoll Associates was
already in place when Florence started working with Hans.
His first catalog had already acknowledged the importance
of design as a differential branding tool for his company.

The Knoll Planning Unit had already been formed, albeit in a different format and with a slightly different purpose than those of what it would become.

> The earliest documented incarnation of the Planning Unit dates to 1944, when Hans Knoll invited "a group of designers with architectural and engineering backgrounds"—Serge Chermayeff, Charles Eames, Antonin and Noémi Raymond, Joe Johannson, Louis Kahn and Oscar Stonorov, Ralph Rapson and Eero Saarinen—to submit furniture designs suitable for mass production. Long before the advent of our current celebrity-obsessed culture, Knoll used famous names to develop and market its designs, a practice the company has continued to the present. The project was coordinated by German-born industrial designer Walter Baermann. Hans Knoll may have met Baermann through Florence Schust (later Florence Knoll) and her connections to the Cranbrook Academy of Art, where Baermann was head of the industrial design department from 1941…Hans Knoll and Walter Baermann envisioned the Planning Unit would form partnerships with manufacturers who had dramatically increased their productive capacities during World War II and needed to find peacetime conversion uses for their factories.[26]

There were three notable responses to this first Planning Unit call. One was Louis I. Kahn's (1901–74) Parasol House Type, a scheme for plywood modular housing that made use of the resources and know-how developed by the aircraft industry during the war (although this wasn't strictly furniture design, it relied on similar manufacturing procedures). The second was a collection of aluminum outdoor furniture and accessories designed by Ralph Rapson (1914–2008), which, again, envisioned an association with the aircraft industry. The third proposal, also by Rapson, was a set of chairs in stamped metal.

None of the designs, however, came to fruition, mostly due to a lack of engagement from the manufacturers the Planning Unit had envisioned to collaborate with.[27]

Hans's business approach was broad and unfocused, which resulted in many of his initiatives being short-lived. Florence Knoll, on the other hand, had acquired, through her distinguished architectural training, a clear vision of what she wanted to do and how she wanted to work. "I was happy to work on the perfection of an idea," she said. "He was for expansion."[28] Her sharp mind and ability to prioritize, more than Hans Knoll's wide-ranging vision, provided the clarity Knoll Associates needed in order to establish a clear direction of business and gain recognition as a leading reference for modernist design.

Hans Knoll, as Florence Knoll remarked, was good at sniffing out all sorts of projects from various clients.[29]

> This was the beginning of the Planning Unit. Our major work was for government commissions related to the war effort. USO's for the troops, USIS for information agencies. I never saw the results of any of these jobs except for the USO in Times Square. After the war, we were asked to design government projects and produce furniture and fabrics in Europe using counterpart dollars. We travelled from Stuttgart to Milan to Paris locating sources for manufacturing the items to be shipped to various destinations for US personnel in devastated areas.[30]

While these projects enabled Florence Knoll to start to develop her design language, they did not contribute a great deal to the consolidation of the Knoll brand. One of the first important Planning Unit projects that pointed to the direction the company would take under Florence Knoll's guidance was the living room of the flat of Howard and Louise Myers (the same couple who had assisted Hans and Jens Risom on their American tour a few years before). Howard Myers was, according to Florence Knoll, "the catalyst of modern architecture and design" in the US. Together with his wife Louise, they "promoted the cause of contemporary furniture and interiors."[31] The Myers threw parties and invited all the high-caliber people linked to the modernist cause. On one of these occasions Florence Knoll's interior design received praise by none less than "severe critic" Frank Lloyd Wright (1867–1959).[32] Another significant early Knoll project, also promoted by the Myers, was the Rockefeller Family Offices at Rockefeller Center, later commended by Nelson Rockefeller "for its rare and effective blending of good taste, originality, and administrative ability."[33] In her collected papers, Florence Knoll remembered a peculiar anecdote about this project:

> I was fortunate to be chosen to design the floor for the Rockefeller brothers in the Rockefeller Center in about 1946. It was one of my first early office projects, and they were wonderful clients. The furniture was custom made of fine woods and materials but everything was low key… Nelson had one request that was to keep his existing inkwell because he liked the pen. The problem was it was made of some plastic like Bakelite and looked very out of place. I solved the problem by calling on my friend Isamu Noguchi to carve a cover for the offending inkwell making a small sculpture of solid English oak. Everyone was happy with this unique piece.[34] (Fig. 2)

Later, the Rockefellers commissioned two other projects from the Knoll Planning Unit, including Nelson Rockefeller's residence and the offices and director's residence of the Rockefeller Institute for Medical Research, now Rockefeller University, in New York. "Sort of starting at the top," Florence Knoll teased.[35] Charismatic and intelligent clients like the

Fig. 2: Rockefeller Family Offices, by Florence Knoll/Knoll Planning Unit, with cover for inkwell by Isamu Noguchi, circa 1946 (Florence Knoll Basset papers, Archives of American Art, Smithsonian Institution)

Myers and the Rockefellers later proved instrumental for Knoll Associates in its quest to convert new clients to its modernist cause. "What this did for us," Knoll recalls, "was that when we made presentations to clients and they said 'Oh, that's far too modern for us,' I could say, 'Well, it certainly isn't too modern for the Rockefellers,' and they would change their minds."[36]

The Knolls were considered to be a fashionable couple, and they both had excellent connections. This certainly helped keep their business afloat in the rather unstable conditions they encountered in the early stages of their journey. As architect and editor Peter Blake (1920–2006) reported:

It all started in 1943, when I first went to work for the *Architectural Forum* as its most junior writer. It was my first assignment, and Howard Myers told me to take a look at some chairs that were about to be produced by H. G. Knoll Associates. The firm, it seemed, was an offshoot of a company that had made early modern furniture in Germany and England in the 1920s and 1930s; and these new chairs were about to be made and distributed by Hans, the original Knoll's son who had come to the US in 1937. The chairs had a form-fitting wood frame and a continuous seat-and-back made out of surplus parachute webbing—one of the few materials available in the civil setting in 1943. "You'll like Hans Knoll, I think," Howard said. As a matter of fact, I wasn't sure I did. I went up to that little showroom at 601 Madison and met Hans, and together we looked at the chairs. The trouble was that Hans was just too beautiful, too charming, too elegant, too blonde, his voice (that Swabian accent, overlaid on European English) just a bit to mellifluous. He was just too much. Well, of course, we became (just about) each other's closest friend. He and Florence Schust (who would later become his wife) and I became almost inseparable. Hans and Shu worked like maniacs, day and night, trying to find ways of designing and manufacturing this or that, squeezing materials out of the war economy, discovering and then supporting young and relatively unknown designers. And whenever Hans and Shu were ready to call it a day—usually around 10 pm—I'd drop by and we would go for a late dinner, or to some nightclub conveniently located on the way back to their apartment in one of those charming, black-and-white-striped houses that used to inhabit Sutton Place. Hans and Shu, in the 1940s, were really at the center of everything that was happening in modern furniture design in America.[37]

Hans Knoll was an impressive character and had great entrepreneurial and social skills. He was, however, perhaps a little too connected with the Europe he had left behind to find the right focus to grow his business. As mentioned above, the government contracts Hans had secured in the early days of the Planning Unit led Knoll Associates to start operating woodworking and textile plants in Italy, France, and Germany. This international expansion, which consolidated in the 1950s, made Hans particularly proud. "It no doubt gave Knoll a great sense of achievement that he was returning to Europe, his birthplace and the birthplace of modernist furniture, with a successful collection of designs that he was manufacturing."[38] People close to Hans Knoll in fact revealed that he sometimes regretted how fast things had happened with Knoll Associates and how big the company had become because, he said, there were other things he might have wanted to do. "Likable as his life in New York might have been," architectural author and Knoll Associates former employee Brian Lutz wrote, he did not discard the idea of returning to Europe one day and starting an enterprise there.[39]

Florence Knoll was more down-to-earth. She understood from the early days that it would be convenient for her company to make alliances with modernist architects who were at the time receiving large commissions from the corporate sector. In this way Knoll Associates could secure a steady intake of work.

> Many early postwar projects of the Planning Unit came through the Knolls' friends and connections. The bulk of the orders came from architects specifying Knoll furniture for their new buildings, so Florence Knoll's extensive contacts from her training at the Cranbrook Academy of Art, the Architectural Association in London, and the Illinois Institute of Technology and particularly from her professional experience in the offices of Marcel Breuer in Cambridge, Massachusetts, and Harrison & Abramovitz in New York City yielded much work.[40]

Wallace K. Harrison was a collaborator in the designs for
the Aluminum Company of America (Alcoa) Offices in
Pittsburgh, realized in collaboration with Eero Saarinen &
Associates (1953), and the Carnegie Endowment for International Peace in New York (1953). With Eero Saarinen, the
Knoll Planning Unit furnished several other projects, as mentioned in Chapter 1. (Fig. 3) As a Knoll advertisement from 1955
established: "The Knoll Planning Unit, design consultants to
the architect, simplifies his task by coordinating interiors with
the total plan. Many noted architects have found this Knoll
service invaluable in a wide range of major projects."[41] Working with modernist architects also brought cultural status and
media exposure to the work of Knoll Associates, as there was,
at the time, a great deal of interest from the press as well as
from different cultural institutions in the language of modern
architecture. While reaching out to architects as potential
collaborators, Florence Knoll also had the vision to extend
her message to the relevant audience beyond the design
community. "As a young company trying to send the message
of modern furniture and interiors, I felt we should advertise
in publications that would reach executive clients. I suggested
using *Fortune* magazine and the *New Yorker*."[42]

Florence Knoll's attitude was both selfless and strategic. In the years at the Architectural Association in London,
through her focus on "learning about construction," she might
have nurtured a hope of practicing as an architect one day.
Yet this hope seems to have faded away quite quickly upon her
return to the US. The fact that she was always assigned to do
interiors in the freelance jobs she took might have been a hint.
It is even possible that she opted for freelancing in the first
place for lack of opportunities for securing permanent work in
the predominantly male working environment of that period.
Operating in an unfavorable setup, despite her good connections and excellent educational credentials, Florence Knoll

had to reduce the scope of her contribution in order to carve out a niche for herself. She fought her way.

> Frazar Wilde [president of the Connecticut General Life
> Insurance Company] was on the fence about whether to go
> traditional or modern, and we did a model for him—according
> to their needs, without thinking about how many square feet.
> When Frazar and his executives saw this, and saw how
> it worked, Frazar said: "Well, you've already paid for all your
> fees by saving all the square footage that we don't need."[43]

In the mid-1950s, Wilde commissioned architecture firm Skidmore, Owings & Merrill (SOM) to design a new campus near Hartford for 3,000 employees, with Isamu Noguchi (1904–88) as the landscape designer.[44] The Knoll Planning Unit got involved at an early stage because of the success of a previous and much smaller collaboration with SOM—the 1947 Madison Room, a restaurant at the Harry S. Manchester Department Store in Madison, Wisconsin. For the Hartford commission, Florence Knoll participated in the creation of a $100,000 one-to-one mock-up of a part of the building prior to construction. The experiment proved that the area of some executive offices could be reduced by as much as thirty percent in relation to what had been initially suggested in the brief.

> Because of the high cost of building, every square foot of space
> must count. Careful arrangement of the furniture units can
> result in a significant saving of space. The object is not to make
> rooms smaller simply to reduce cost but to make them the size
> they reasonably should be to fulfill their function. Even in the
> most economically planned building some of the areas should
> have a sense of spaciousness for visual counterpoint to a series
> of small rooms.[45]

Fig. 3: Alcoa Offices, Pittsburgh, interior design by Florence Knoll/ Knoll Planning Unit, architecture by Harrison & Abramovitz with Eero Saarinen & Associates, 1953 (Courtesy of Knoll Archives)

Florence Knoll not only had to prove her skills in space planning, showing clients how they could save space without doing away with the image of prosperity they needed to convey. But she also had to hit the right buttons in relation to the modernist design orientation that was in vogue at the time. SOM partner Gordon Bunshaft, who ran the Connecticut General Life Insurance Company project, recalled:

> Shu Knoll had developed quite an interior department and she was hired to do the interiors at our recommendation. It was a very happy joint venture. Our design interests were more or less the same: International Modern.[46] (Plate 9, Figs. 4–5)

Florence Knoll understood that, in order to convince her clients about her innovative ideas, she had to develop an efficient and appealing way to communicate them. "Just looking at a blueprint, for most clients, does not work," she argued. "They don't know what they are looking at."[47] Knoll mitigated the abstract dryness of technical drawings with her paste-ups, which gave a good sense of the materiality of the spaces she was creating. In order to demonstrate the effectiveness of her layout proposals, she often made use of large three-dimensional scale models.

The campus of Connecticut General Life Insurance Company was designed under the assumption that "a good place to work means attractive recreation space as well as efficient offices."[48] The Knoll Planning Unit was in charge

Above, Fig. 4: Board of directors' lounge, Connecticut General Life Insurance Company Offices, Hartford, interior design by Florence Knoll/Knoll Planning Unit, architecture by Skidmore, Owings and Merrill, photograph by Ezra Stoller, circa 1950s (Courtesy of Knoll Archives); **Below, Fig. 5:** Executive office, Connecticut General Life Insurance Company Offices, Hartford, interior design by Florence Knoll/Knoll Planning Unit, architecture by Skidmore, Owings and Merrill, photograph by Ezra Stoller, circa 1950s (Courtesy of Knoll Archives)

of securing the right atmosphere for each space so the experience would be flawless and conducive to the success of the business.

> Connecticut General's own employees are living incredibly well at work, swaddled in space, surrounded by art and conveniences: bowling alleys, tennis courts, shop, a magnificent eating place. This has its business point too. The population of workers is mostly young girls eagerly courted by many companies in the area and the building has already begun to weigh well as an added attraction.[49]

At Connecticut General, Florence Knoll did a great job of furnishing the modern office, finding fairly humanized solutions for the rather sterile modularity of the modernist building and seamlessly playing the corporate game. In this and in other projects, she paid a considerable contribution to the design of the "American workplace, where women, who largely played supportive roles, were visible in the open-plan configurations, but invisible within the corporations' higher ranks."[50] Florence Knoll prided herself for having improved the typical secretarial desk, customizing the design of this and other furniture based on interviews the Planning Unit team conducted with employees from all levels. In her determination to do her job properly, she sometimes failed to understand, however, that improving functionality was not always sufficient to boost the working conditions and well-being of the workers. The design language Knoll employed was no doubt coercive enough to attract good employees, selling to them as well as to clients and investors the image of a solid and reliable, yet also hip and smart, organization. Yet this did not necessarily impact positively on the quality of the working relationships or environment.

Connecticut General was an exemplary model of total design. Its interiors were perfectly streamlined with the architecture, providing a smooth, coherent experience. Remarkably, the color scheme of this interior is gayer and livelier than in most other Knoll offices, which no doubt helped the company sell the idea that working with them was fun and exciting.

After completing the Connecticut General project, Florence Knoll fell out with SOM partner Gordon Bunshaft, as they disagreed on issues around the publicity and credits of the work. "We worked so closely that Shu thought she had done the building for a while," he wrote.[51] Acclaimed and successful as this project was, Florence Knoll nonetheless reveals in her collected papers that it did not correspond necessarily to the line of work she found most enjoyable and stimulating for creating interiors.

> In reviewing my work over the years, I find that I really enjoyed the challenge of difficult design problems to be found in older buildings as opposed to more modern modular construction. A case in point was the renovation of the CBS offices [1952–54] on Madison Avenue. They were located in an older building that presented innumerable problems such as awkward structural situations, poor fenestration and other disadvantages. Struggling with them created interesting design results…One example was the reception room. It had an awkwardly placed single window in the corner of the wall. Using wall color, a translucent curtain and special furniture, I was able to create an interesting abstraction.[52] (Figs. 6, 7)

The solutions Florence Knoll found for refurbishing existing spaces were, at times, more complex and meticulous than the interiors she designed for new buildings. At CBS, although the general design orientation verged, in tandem with the

Fig. 6: President's office, Columbia Broadcasting Systems (CBS) Offices, New York, by Florence Knoll/Knoll Planning Unit, photograph by Yuichi Idaka, 1952–4 (Courtesy of Knoll Archives)

principle of total design, toward an overall sense of coherence, particular elements, such as the above-mentioned "awkwardly placed window," created some tension, lending more individuality to the scheme. Another challenge this commission posed was the need to conceal a sophisticated electronic control system, which included phonograph, telephone, radio, and televisions. For this, Knoll reverted to the streamlined way of thinking that characterized the Planning Unit, creating an ingenious storage unit to resolve the problem, which she detailed in an elaborate but concise sketch. (Fig. 8) Drawings

Fig. 7: Reception room, Columbia Broadcasting Systems (CBS) Offices, New York, by Florence Knoll/Knoll Planning Unit, photograph by Yuichi Idaka, 1952–4 (Courtesy of Knoll Archives)

such as this one is evidence, once again, one of the main hallmarks of the Knoll look: the articulation of an utilitarian problem with such a degree of care and artistry that it almost acquired, in itself, a decorative status. At CBS, Knoll balanced moments of extreme precision, as in the electronic control unit, with ones where some improvisation was employed, as in the above-mentioned window. This made her design language more nuanced and created a less-uniform interior in comparison, for instance, to the previously discussed Connecticut General project.

Florence Knoll established an excellent relationship
with CBS's president Frank Stanton (1908–2006). She
revealed they selected all the artwork for the CBS interior
together and that she had designed his office as a special hom-
age to his "particular and refined style."[53] This relationship
led to another Knoll Planning Unit project: Look Publications
Offices in New York (1962), again a refurbishment of an existing structure. (Figs.9, 10) A contemporary article highlighted the
cunning solution of separating the executive offices from the
secretarial area, which brought to the space "an atmosphere
of pervasive calm."[54] It also praised the Knoll Planning Unit's
smart proposition of concealing nearly all structural columns
in bookcases and storage walls. "In two instances, a narrow
storage closet has been planned between offices instead
of leaving a column freestanding within one of the rooms."[55]
It took an enormous amount of work to nail down every
detail of this project:

> The number of drawings executed for the project is another
> indication of KPU's [Knoll Planning Unit] precision. Beside
> the usual plans—construction, electrical, plumbing, heating-
> ventilation-air conditioning, and finishing and furniture
> plans—and several preliminary sketches, KPU also executed
> plans and schedules for floor coverings, draperies and blinds,
> plants, pictures and accessories. Details and working draw-
> ings of special furniture brought the total number of drawings
> for these offices to 197. The interior designers also used other
> planning materials: a model of the major areas was built, and a
> "paste-up," which is a furniture plan with textiles pasted over
> the designated areas, was used as a portable model.[56]

If in the CBS project Florence Knoll chose to take advantage
of the inconsistencies of the existing building, turning them
into design features, at Look Publications she hid them as

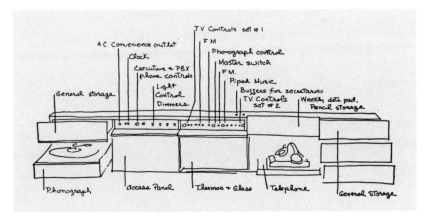

Fig. 8: Sketch of cabinet for the office of the president, Columbia
Broadcasting Systems (CBS) Offices, New York, by Florence Knoll/Knoll
Planning Unit, 1952–54 (Florence Knoll Basset papers, Archives
of American Art, Smithsonian Institution)

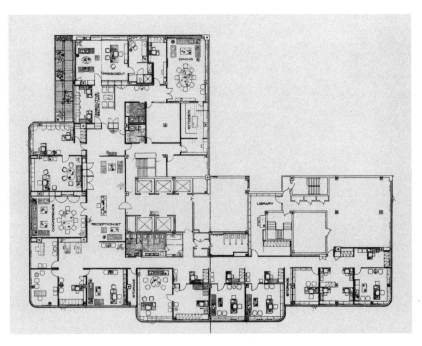

Fig. 9: Plan of Look Publications Offices, New York, by Florence Knoll/
Knoll Planning Unit, 1962 (Florence Knoll Basset papers, Archives of
American Art, Smithsonian Institution)

Fig. 10: Executive lounge and dining area,
Look Publications Offices, New York,
by Florence Knoll/Knoll Planning Unit, 1962
(Courtesy of Knoll Archives)

much as possible, resulting in a more precise and controlled but less particular interior.

Whether she was playing with or avoiding inconsistencies, Florence Knoll took the level of finesse and precision that would be expected of a theatrical set, a church, an art museum, or a gallery to the office space, making the "arrangements comfortable looking and rather residential in character."[57] Her attention to detail added substantially to the persuasive nature of her work, which changed in character according to each project. In some interiors, like at Connecticut General, the persuasive character of the design was focused on the notion of well-being and on the alignment of work with entertainment. "While game rooms, coffee and nap rooms may be enjoyable, these spaces also function as a means to tap onto unpaid wage hours of employees, getting them to work longer hours in exchange for having a 'cool' workplace."[58] In others, like at CBS, she associated the sense of enticement of the interior to ideas of sophistication rather than fun.

"Pleasurable offices remained a symbol of status, and thus an element of desire," communications and new media researcher Renyi Hong argued. In "one aspect, the fantasy of the office related to the fantasy of meritocracy."[59] Elegant offices like Frank Stanton's at CBS gave workers something to aspire toward. "Closeness to beautiful offices amplified the belief that such pleasures could be available to all through hard work."[60] This was something Florence Knoll might have personally related to: fighting through hard work for deserved success and recognition and for the compensations that came with it. While complying within the slightly cynical framework of corporate thinking, Knoll seems, nevertheless, to have found a way to be sincere and, through her designs, to promote something she might have genuinely believed in and thought to be possible based on her own experience.[61]

Relating to Florence Knoll's discreet personality, the refined character of interiors like the CBS communicated a certain sense of dignity, which contrasted with the more permissive atmosphere experienced in spaces like the Connecticut General complex. It is possible that these circumspect qualities might also have encouraged a more respectful working behavior—unlike what was depicted in the previously discussed television series *Mad Men*.

Sophistication was, again, one of the themes of the second project Florence Knoll did for the CBS company, this time in a new building designed by her friend Eero Saarinen. The CBS Headquarters in New York (1964), the last scheme Florence Knoll designed with the Planning Unit, consisted of a new, thirty-eight-floor building expected to house 2,700 employees, with none less than 868 offices divided into four different types. Saarinen originally intended to design the interiors himself— with Knoll's help, he told her over dinner—but upon his death in 1961 the Planning Unit took over.

The overall strategy Florence Knoll adopted for the design of these CBS interiors was similar to the one used in her previous projects.

> The aim of Mrs Bassett [Florence Knoll's name after 1958] in doing the interiors of the 35 floors of the CBS building devoted to offices was a degree of pleasant concealment, a goal stemming from her belief that "the simpler the background, the easier the thought process." This was accomplished in general clerical areas, while making full use of the 35 feet of free space around the core, by separating functions with banks of lateral filing cabinets...Office supplies, stored on each floor, are concealed behind folding doors, immediately above. Ten-foot offices for staff are interrupted by open secretarial bays. Steel furniture in the building is from Art Metal, which worked closely with the systems staff of CBS and Mrs Bassett to meet functional needs.[62]

The goal throughout was simplicity. This was achieved through methodical and efficient design procedures, in addition to the solutions outlined above, such as mounting light switches in door jambs; concealing telephones, control panels, and other special equipment completely from view; color coding the reception area of each floor to indicate its overall color scheme; and choosing fabrics and other materials not only for their visual effect but also for their acoustic performance. (Plate 7)

The highlights of the scheme were, however, the executive suites. For those, Florence Knoll introduced a more subtle color scheme, composed of metallic browns and olive greens. Textiles included lush velvets, until then an uncommon material in her palette. And the Knoll Planning Unit even designed different sets of pleats for the curtains:

> To avoid the traditional French pleat that is much overworked on traverse draperies today, Knoll Planning Unit developed "a pleatless pleat" for the vice-presidential offices. "It was devised to minimize the appearance of the pleat and to integrate the softness of the fabrics into the appearance of the pleating technique." The Knoll Planning Unit also designed a pleat for the corporate presidential suites. It uses continuous box pleats, therefore yards of fabric, and is grandly luxurious. Here are two thoughtful variations on the common traverse drapery that prove how imagination can expand and rejuvenate tradition.[63]

Knoll's "pleatless pleat" for the vice-presidential suite made the room look more casual and simpler, in harmony with many of Knoll's earlier interventions. In the presidential suites, however, she went for a more imposing, more traditional-looking draping style aligned with the more old-fashioned colors and textures she was experimenting

Fig. 11: Frank Stanton's private dining room, Columbia Broadcasting Systems (CBS) Offices, New York, interior design by Florence Knoll/ Knoll Planning Unit, architecture by Eero Saarinen & Associates, 1964 (Florence Knoll Basset papers, Archives of American Art, Smithsonian Institution)

with.[64] In the private dining room of Frank Stanton's suite on the thirty-fifth floor, Knoll introduced other unmodern details: a pair of Tiffany glass panels "set in the standard windows in front of translucent glass with back lighting to provide a consistent glow of light."[65] (Fig. 11)

As the CBS Headquarters indicates, Florence Knoll started to engage a less homogeneous design language in later moments of her career at Knoll Associates, moving away from an orthodox form of modernism and sometimes introducing historical elements into her vocabulary. Consequentially, the message conveyed by her interiors also changed, as a richer and more inclusive repertoire replaced a predominantly abstract and self-referential language. In Knoll's later projects, the decorative aspects of the design no longer related exclusively to the realm of the utilitarian. This also meant that they diverted from celebrating exclusively work-related values to pointing to a wider reality, which started to include also the world outside the office. Knoll's later interiors continued to be coercive, yet, rather than emphasize an ideology of work for work's sake (or for financial compensation), they promised something different. Elements such as the Tiffany glass panels and the more luxurious pleats and fabrics she employed in the CBS design connected the user to ideas of pleasure, leisure, meaning, and comfort that were not mediated by the yardstick of efficiency and not directly circumscribed by the corporate way of thinking. Although in most cases such transformations were still contrived—standing alongside pristine white walls, built-in ceiling lights, sleek furniture, and the usually rather rigid Knoll layout—they indicate nonetheless a departure from the Knoll look as it had been established in the preceding years. Their design language was more akin to the one that Florence Knoll would develop in the works she did after she left Knoll Associates.

While promoting the rather formulaic Knoll look, Florence Knoll took some liberties. In some cases—like in the first CBS project—she was prompted by the peculiarities of the physical context in which she was operating. In other situations, Knoll's incursions outside of the modernist canon were influenced by other designers. In the early 1950s, when Knoll Associates started to set foot in Europe, Knoll International was founded. The company subsequently established showrooms in Paris (1951), Stuttgart (1952), and Milan (1956), as well as in many other capitals in Europe and worldwide. The main contact the Knolls had in France was a man named Yves Vidal (1923–2001) —on account of their common collaboration with the US State Department. With his partner, interior decorator Charles Sévigny (1918–2019), Vidal had been in charge of renovating American ambassadorial residences throughout Europe. They formed a partnership in 1951, and Vidal was appointed president of Knoll International in 1955.

In line with the tradition of interior decoration, Vidal and Sévigny did not abide to the logic of total design. Rather, they freely combined modern with period styles, and Western with non-Western influences in idiosyncratic and flamboyant settings. Around the same time Knoll was working on the CBS Headquarters, Vidal and Sévigny started to use their own homes—one in Saint-Maurice, France and the other in Tangiers, Morocco—as branding tools for their design style. They combined some of Knoll Associates' iconic pieces with a varied range of antiques and ornaments and placed them against period architecture. (Fig. 12) Their look was very popular, and it contributed a great deal to the dissemination of the Knoll products to the European as well as to other markets, where they tended to be employed in residential more than in office environments.[66] It is likely that Florence Knoll was inspired by Sévigny and Vidal's designs, although she never openly admitted to this. She used similar combinations of

Fig. 12: York Castle, Tangier, Morocco, by Charles Sévigny and Yves Vidal, circa 1960 (Courtesy of Knoll Archives)

Fig. 13: Bassett suite waiting room, Southeast Bank, Miami, interior design by Florence Knoll, architecture by Skidmore, Owings and Merrill, 1982 (Florence Knoll Basset papers, Archives of American Art, Smithsonian Institution)

Knoll furniture with non-modernist features in, besides the CBS Headquarters, her two private houses as well as in a corporate interior for the Southeast Bank, Miami (1982), which she designed after retiring from Knoll Associates. (Fig. 13) It is telling that Knoll chose to flirt with established notions of femininity and let herself be influenced by a look associated with the lifestyle of a gay couple (Vidal and Sévigny) when she was about to leave Knoll Associates (CBS Headquarters) and when she no longer relied on her design and entrepreneurial work at the company to make a living or build her professional reputation (Knoll Bassett Houses 1 and 2 and Southeast Bank schemes).

NOTES

1. Video Interview with Florence Knoll, 1998 (Cranbrook Archives, Detroit).

2. Lutz, *Knoll*, 11.

3. Ibid. The Deutscher Werkbund was influenced by the Arts and Crafts tradition—which had influenced Florence Knoll's design education in Cranbrook—in its intention to improve the quality of everyday design and products. It was, however, generally more open to acknowledging the possible benefits of engaging industrial production. Also, while the English movement employed rather diffuse methods of dissemination for its ideas and design ethics—which included schools, guilds, and other types of associations that were not necessarily in conversation with one another—the German venture was more structured and organized. Consumer education was one the priorities of the Werkbund. As design curator Matilda McQuaid explains, the organization enlisted "retailers as agents of reform. Lectures were organized in order to educate the shopkeepers, who ultimately affected consumers through the choice and presentation of products. The Werkbund sponsored a campaign to improve the quality of window displays in stores, reasoning that the shop window is the most practical means of educating both the retailer and the public at large. The Werkbund also made use of German museums to influence public taste, and by 1913 its board included ten museum directors. In 1909 the Deutsches Museum für Kunst in Handel und Gewerbe in Hagen became the primary organizer of Werkbund exhibitions, in effect, the Werkbund Museum." Matilda McQuaid, *Lilly Reich: Designer and Architect* (New York: Museum of Modern Art, 1995), 10, 13. See also Joan Campbell, *The German Werkbund: The Politics of Reform in the Applied Arts* (Princeton: Princeton University Press, 1978). The strategies used by the Deutscher Werkbund to disseminate the modernist language were mirrored in the US in the mid twentieth century, with important art institutions—like the Museum of Modern Art (MoMA) in New York—supporting the cause and helping organize fairs, exhibitions and competitions. See, for instance, Susan Ward, "The Design, Promotion, and Production of Modern Textiles in the USA, 1940–60," in Martin, *Knoll Textiles*, 36–73.

4. Lutz, *Knoll*, 14.
5. See "Walter Knoll / Wilhelm Knoll," Manufacturers & Makers, Pamono, accessed May 28, 2018, https://www.pamono.co.uk/makers/walter-knoll-wilhelm-knoll.
6. Lutz, *Knoll*, 14.
7. See "Walter Knoll / Wilhelm Knoll."
8. See "Walter Knoll—The Furniture Brand of Modernity," History, About Walter Knoll, Walter Knoll, accessed May 28, 2018, https://www.walterknoll.de/en/about/history/history.
9. See Makovsky, "Knoll before Knoll Textiles," 74.
10. Walter Knoll & Co. acquired the Wilhelm Knoll Company in the 1980s. It has been in the market for nearly a hundred years, having accumulated an impressive portfolio, including outfitting the Berlin Tegel Airport in the 1970s and collaborations with architect-designers such as Norman Foster (b. 1935) and Pearson Lloyd (est. 1997). It currently has a subsidiary in Australia and showrooms in London, Paris, Mumbai, and Beijing.
11. Larrabee and Vignelli, *Knoll Design*, 18.
12. Chermayeff—who, in fact, had no formal architectural training—had in the 1930s formed a collaboration with the German expressionist designer Erich Mendelsohn (1887–1953). They together designed the acclaimed De La Warr Pavilion in Bexhill-on-Sea, England. Years later Chermayeff moved to the US and devoted his career to academia, presiding the Institute of Design in Chicago from 1946 to 1951, and teaching at MIT, Yale, and Harvard, among other schools. For more information on him, see Alan Powers, "Obituary: Serge Chermayeff," *Independent*, May 14, 1996, accessed May 28, 2018, https://www.independent.co.uk/incoming/obituary-serge-chermayeff-5616070.html.
13. Makovsky, "Knoll before Knoll Textiles," 76.
14. Larrabee and Vignelli, *Knoll Design*, 18.
15. See Arnold and Puff, "Knoll Look," 191.
16. Lutz, *Knoll*, 17.
17. Ibid., 18.
18. Ibid., 20–21.
19. Makovsky, "Knoll before Knoll Textiles," 77.
20. Miller ran a fashionable furnishings and textile store in New York that represented "the new generation of American designers." See Alastair Gordon, *Weekend Utopia: Modern Living in the Hamptons* (New York: Princeton Architectural Press, 2001), 36. Her rugs and textiles were included in a number of exhibitions, including the International Exposition in Paris from 1937 (where she was awarded a gold medal for Decorative Textiles). She also became known for commissioning a progressive and innovative modernist house by the beach in Southampton, New York, that she dubbed the Sandbox (1933). See Makovsky, "Knoll before Knoll Textiles," 100n42.
21. Lutz, *Knoll*, 22.
22. The company was founded in 1941 under the name of "Harrison, Fouilhoux & Abramovitz." It changed its name to "Harrison, Abramovitz & Abbe" after Fouilhoux's death in 1945, and years later it was again renamed "Harrison, Abramovitz & Harris." Today, its legacy is more commonly associated with the name of "Harrison & Abramovitz." See "Harrison & Abramovitz," in Eva Franch i Gilabert et al., eds., *OfficeUS: Atlas* (Zurich: Lars Muller, 2015), 156–7.
23. Warren, "Woman Who Led Office."
24. See Makovsky, "Knoll before Knoll Textiles," 77 and 101n91.
25. See Larrabee and Vignelli, *Knoll Design*, 20.
26. Tigerman, "Heart and Soul," 180–1.
27. See Lutz, *Knoll*, 60–61.
28. Janet Chusmir, "Florence Bassett's World on Display," *Miami Herald*, March 12, 1972.
29. Tigerman, "Heart and Soul," 184.
30. "Biographical Material," 13.
31. Larrabee and Vignelli, *Knoll Design*, 20.
32. "Letters," Folder 2, 24.
33. Ibid.
34. "Subject Files," Folder 5, 54.
35. Chusmir, "Florence Bassett's World."
36. Maeve Slavin, "Aesthetic Revolutionary," *Working Woman* (January 1984), 76.
37. Blake, *No Place Like Utopia*, 171–72. Blake refers to a Knoll Showroom at 601 Madison Avenue that predates the 1948 configuration presented in the last chapter of this book.
38. Lutz, *Knoll*, 62.
39. Ibid.
40. See Tigerman, "Heart and Soul," 184.
41. Ibid., 192.
42. "Subject Files," Folder 7, 4.
43. Lutz, *Knoll*, 32.
44. See "Skidmore, Owings & Merrill," in Franch i Gilabert et al., OfficeUS, 214–15.
45. Larrabee and Vignelli, *Knoll Design*, 80.
46. Lutz, *Knoll*, 34.
47. Ibid., 49.
48. "Connecticut General Life Insurance Company Press Release," circa 1950s, Knoll Archives.
49. "Insurance Sets a Pattern," *Architectural Forum* (September 1957), 114.

50. Hilary Sample, "Natalie de Blois," in
Eva Franch i Gilbert, et al., eds., *OfficeUS:
Agenda* (Zurich: Lars Muller, 2014), 67.
Natalie de Blois, a director at SOM, was,
incidentally, another woman who was closely
involved in the design of the Connecticut
General Life Insurance Company Offices,
having been most notably in charge of the
common areas and landscaping. Like Knoll,
de Blois "helped develop the modern style,"
which included the re-engineering of "the
workspace of (largely women) secretaries."
(Ibid., 65).
51. Lutz, *Knoll*, 294n46. Some years later
SOM started its own interior design division.
52. "Subject Files," Folder 17, 2.
53. Tigerman, "Heart and Soul," 192.
54. "Model of Office Planning," *Interior
Design Data* (March 1962): 151.
55. Ibid., 153.
56. Ibid.
57. Ibid.
58. Hong, "Office Interiors," 545–46.
59. Ibid., 551.
60. Ibid.
61. Knoll's advantaged social condition has
certainly played a significant part in her
successful professional journey. She probably
would not have become a partner at Knoll
Associates, for example, had she not bailed
out Hans using her inheritance money. She
might not even have gone to Cranbrook or
studied at the Architectural Association in
London had she been less privileged. Still,
given the extremely difficult conditions she
was confronted with, her career ascension
was noteworthy all the same.
62. "The Interiors at CBS" (unauthored),
Office Design (May 1966).
63. Ibid.
64. Knoll's use of curtains and materials in
this project was clearly influenced by the
interior design style of Mies van der Rohe and
Lilly Reich. See, for example, Schuldenfrei,
"Subjectivity: Mies van der Rohe's Materiality
and the Reinscribing of Modernism's
Meaning" in *Luxury and Modernism*, 157–222.
65. "Biographical Material," 81.
66. There was a precedent for Sévigny's
and Vidal's idiosyncratic combination of
modernist and period styles through the use
of contrasting furniture: the interiors of the
governmental palaces in the new Brazilian
capital, Brasília. "Whereas the European
modern movement at first demanded a
complete break with cultural tradition, the
Brazilian movement legitimized the country's
modernity by evoking tradition. This is also
the reason the baroque art of the gold mining
region and the folk art were considered
manifestations of the Brazilian spirit and
genuine expressions of national identity."
Luciana Saboia, Elane Ribeiro Peixoto, and
José Airton Costa Junior, "National Identity
and Modern Furniture in Brasília's Itamaraty
Palace," in Fredie Floré and Cammie McAtee,
eds., *The Politics of Furniture: Identity,
Diplomacy and Persuasion in Post-War
Interiors* (London: Routledge, 2017), 140 and
Cammie McAtee and Fredie Floré, "Knolling
Paris: From the 'New Look' to *Knoll au
Louvre*" in Floré and McAtee, *Politics of
Furniture*, 98–118.

CHAPTER THREE:
THE KNOLL ENTERPRISE

"I wanted a chair that was like a basket full of pillows. Well, it didn't quite turn out that way, but I wanted something I could curl up in."[1] That was Florence Knoll's request that prompted Eero Saarinen to design the Womb Chair, a Knoll classic, in 1948. Knoll observed that it was typical of women to try to "curl up" when sitting on a chair. What she probably had in mind was a cozy, soft, informal piece of furniture. What she got instead was a lounge chair that, if it did not entirely restrict the act of curling up, did not fully encourage it either. (See Plate 1)

The material and formal research that led to the design of the Womb Collection started in 1940, when Saarinen collaborated with Charles Eames on some chair designs for the *Organic Design in Home Furnishings* competition organized by the Museum of Modern Art (MoMA) in New York. This was the first of many competitions MoMA organized "to discover good designers and engage them in the task of creating a better environment for today's living."[2] Following the contest, the museum promised to take charge of arranging contracts between the winners and manufacturers. Although Eames's and Saarinen's chairs were winning entries, they did not go into production. The technique they employed was very innovative and, partially owing to the disruptions of World War II, there were not, at that time, manufacturers that could produce their work.[3] MoMA organized an exhibition of the winning pieces in 1941, and its

Fig. 1: Bistrot No. 14, by Michel Thonet, produced by the Thonet Brothers, photograph by Jean-Claude Planchet, 1870 (Musee National d'Art Moderne, Centre Georges Pompidou, Paris, © CNAC/MNAM/Dist. RMN-Grand Palais / Art Resource, NY)

catalog provided an "outline of the development of modern furniture."[4] It started with English designer William Morris (1834–96), who had "taken a major step in his insistence that art and design must be a normal part of life."[5] His work was followed by that of Thonet, a German manufacturer known for its bentwood furniture:

> A second aspect of design is contributed, often unconsciously, by men who, while working with materials and new machines find new forms and new ways of making things. Technicians, engineers, men experimenting with new machine processes—*these are the untrained but instinctive creators of new forms and of a kind of expression which stems directly from materials and methods of manufacture, and is determined by the requirements of use and efficiency.* With no primary intent to create beauty, new beauty is revealed. In this way, little by little, a new esthetic has been born. As an example, *a significant step in furniture design was*

Fig. 2: Paimio Chair, by Alvar Aalto, photograph by Jean-Claude Planchet, 1930–31 (Musee National d'Art Moderne, Centre Georges Pompidou, Paris, © CNAC/MNAM/Dist. RMN-Grand Palais / Art Resource, NY)

taken in 1830 with the invention by Thonet of wood bending which opened up a new esthetic development through a new technical possibility.[6] (Fig. 1)

The catalog—like other modernist texts—praised works that had a sense that technical parameters were leading the way.

Another important step in the "development of modern furniture," as the catalog shows, was the work of Finnish architect Alvar Aalto, who furthered the Thonet idea by adapting it to the technology of bent plywood:

> The single sheet of plywood, which daringly and dramatically forms the seat and back, varies in thickness according to the structural requirements. At the seat, where the weight of the body exerts more strain on the plywood span, additional interior plies are added, thickening the sheet at this point to give more strength.[7]

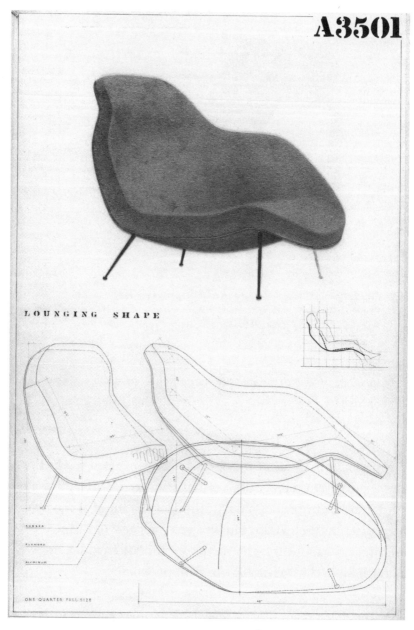

Fig. 3: Armchair submitted for the *Organic Design in Home Furnishings* competition, by Charles Eames and Eero Saarinen, 1940 (The Museum of Modern Art, New York, NY, U.S.A. Digital Image © The Museum of Modern Art/Licensed by SCALA / Art Resource, NY)

Eames and Saarinen's designs were inspired by Aalto's. They used similar principles, but while the seat of his chair was formed through bending the plywood in one single direction, the geometry of the shell of Eames and Saarinen's designs were made more complex by using a compound curvature. (Figs. 2, 3)

Although the pieces by Aalto and by the duo Saarinen and Eames looked like armchairs, their designs were actually much closer to those of side chairs—changed only slightly to give the body more support:

> In an ordinary chair there are a seat and a back which support the body at two or three points. In the case of a usual large upholstered chair the body sinks into a general softness until it reaches support. The principle in these chairs by Saarinen is that of continuous contact and support, with a thin rubber pad for softness at all points.[8]

Because of the reduced softness of the Womb Chair in comparison to that of an armchair structured on a traditional spring system, the body could never really "sink" into the Saarinen chair as Florence Knoll had envisaged when she requested "a chair that was like a basket full of pillows." This was another compromise, where her initial vision was weakened in favour of adjusting to the precepts of the modernist design language. The replacement of soft, bulky padding with much less squishy foam rubber, a consequence of the designer's desire to simplify the furniture in order to "honestly" communicate the technique behind its construction, implied a radical decrease on the level of comfort and relaxation these pieces could provide. Modernism, it turned out, was more about the image of comfort than about comfort itself.[9]

The orientation that guided the design and manufacturing of the Womb Chair—a slight variation of Eames and

Fig. 4: Pedestal Collection, by Eero Saarinen, 1957 (Florence Knoll Basset papers, Archives of American Art, Smithsonian Institution)

Saarinen's designs for MoMA discussed above—was generally followed in other similar furniture pieces produced by Knoll Associates in Florence Knoll's time. Iconic Knoll furniture, like Italian-born Harry Bertoia's Diamond Chair (1953) and Warren Platner's Platner Chair (1966), perform very similarly to the design Eames and Saarinen submitted to the MoMA competition, providing an intermediate level of comfort between an ordinary chair and a traditional padded armchair. Smartly, Knoll Associates labeled these designs "lounge chairs," averting a direct comparison with the generally more cushioned and comfortable "armchairs" while implying their performance was comparable.

The Knolls went to great lengths of effort and dedication to devise and produce their innovative designs, always having in mind that their ultimate goal was to produce new "classics." A 1957 reporter noted, "Few items are dropped from the catalog, and then only for specific reasons, not part of a policy of obsolescence."[10] Knoll products, the company suggested, did not follow fashion trends. They were envisioned instead as long-standing modern substitutes for older models of furniture.

And so it not surprising that the process of Bertoia creating the Diamond Chair for Knoll took over two years. After specializing in metalwork and jewelry at Cranbrook Academy of Art, where he had met Florence Knoll (as discussed in Chapter Two), Bertoia went to work with Charles and Ray Eames in Los Angeles. He contributed to some of their furniture designs but believed he was not properly credited for this. The experience disappointed him, and he eventually left. On a visit to California in 1950, Hans and Florence approached him and offered him a job. "Bertoia's assignment was very open: to go work in his own way, and if he came up with a piece of furniture, so much the better."[11] Hans Knoll suggested Bertoia do some field research—visiting places to see contemporary furniture—but Bertoia felt that ideas should come from an "inward direction."[12]

So Bertoia moved to southeastern Pennsylvania, where the Knoll factory had opened in 1950, took over a room there, and started to work. During the summer, the Knolls visited from New York on weekends. Bertoia recalled, "They were sources of inspiration in many ways; my relationship with both was quite wonderful."[13] Bertoia experimented on his own for about six months, after which the Knolls sent over some product developers to help. It was not, however, until 1953 that prototypes actually started to be produced.[14] The team came up with a highly original collection and also with a special technique required for manufacturing the pieces. When the Diamond Collection was finally launched, it was a triumph. Remarkably, some of its pieces continue to be produced to this day, using the same process Bertoia and his team devised. Following his successful experience with the Knolls, Bertoia remained in Pennsylvania working independently, mainly as a metal sculptor.

A few years after the design of the Womb Chair, Knoll Associates made another deal with Eero Saarinen, which ultimately resulted in the development of the highly acclaimed Pedestal Collection (1958). Saarinen's design intention for this work, he said, was to "clear up the slum of legs," as he thought that the "undercarriage of chairs and tables in a typical interior makes an ugly, confusing, unrestful world."[15] Aware that Saarinen had become one of the most prominent architects working in the US and that he therefore had an immense workload, Hans Knoll asked one of his best product developers to relocate to Michigan and work full-time with him on this new assignment. After nearly two years, they came back with the first handmade glass-fiber-reinforced plastic prototypes. Like the launch of the Womb series, that of the Pedestal line was a success. (Fig. 4) It was praised even by George Nelson (1908–86), design director of Hermann Miller—Knoll Associates' fiercest competitor. Legend has it that upon seeing the Pedestal Chair, Nelson, who was presumably working with Charles Eames on a similar idea, had to give in and admit: this time the Knolls had won.[16]

Hans Knoll's father, Walter Knoll, had manufactured some of Mies van der Rohe's furniture designs in the early 1930s. The German manufacturers Thonet had also

produced some of his chairs in the late 1920s.[17] During
World War II, however, the European production of his
pieces had been completely halted. Upon his arrival in the
US in the late 1930s, Mies was, similarly, unsuccessful in
finding the means to take his furniture back into production. Therefore, when his former student Florence Knoll
approached him to collaborate with Knoll Associates in
the mid 1940s, it probably did not take a lot of convincing.
Remarkably, she suggested some design variations on some
of his classic pieces. For the Brno Chair, in addition to producing the original tubular piece from 1930, she suggested a
version with a structure in rolled metal following the more
refined-looking structure of Mies's Barcelona Chair (1929).
(Figs. 5 and 6) Knoll continues to produce both versions of the
Brno Chair as well as many other Mies designs.

Florence Knoll's own furniture design was, similar to
her interiors, greatly inspired by the work of Eero and Mies.
For the Rockefeller Family Offices at Rockefeller Center
(1946), for example, she created a chair with a curved seat
using the same principle of Eames and Saarinen's pieces for
the *Organic Design* competition. As she reported:

> I knew exactly what I wanted even though it was one of
> the first office jobs I did. *I liked the idea of a chair's arms and
> back being one continuous curve, encircling and supporting the
> occupant*, but the only chairs like this I could find were all
> wood. I wanted to have upholstery on the arms of the chair
> for this project, more for a sense of luxury, rather than
> just having open wood arms.[18]

Interestingly, Eero Saarinen later borrowed from the design
of this chair to create his Model 71 Chair, which "went on to
become Knoll's most significant piece of furniture in its mass
appeal for use in corporate interiors."[19]

Left, Fig. 5: Brno Chair, tubular, original version, by Mies van der Rohe, produced by Berliner Metallgewerbe Joseph Müller, 1930 (The Museum of Modern Art, New York, NY, U.S.A. Digital Image © The Museum of Modern Art/Licensed by SCALA / Art Resource, NY); **Right, Fig. 6:** Brno Chair, flat bar, modified version, by Mies van der Rohe, produced by Knoll Associates, circa 1950s (The Museum of Modern Art, New York, NY, U.S.A. Digital Image © The Museum of Modern Art/Licensed by SCALA / Art Resource, NY)

The most popular furniture work by Florence Knoll was not, however, derived from her Rockefeller Chair. It was, rather, a line inspired by Mies's work, named the Parallel Bar Collection (1954). Originally created for the Connecticut General Offices, its seating frame was inspired by the Barcelona Chair, while its leg structure was more simple, straightforward, and neutral, composed of square-section steel bars riveted together. As Bobbye Tigerman writes:

> The likeness of form and function, and the similar uses to which both lounge chairs were put in Planning Unit interiors, suggest that Florence Knoll may have designed the *Parallel Bar* lounge chair as a less expensive and less conspicuous version of the *Barcelona* chair.[20]

Parallel Bar seating pieces used a particular upholstering technique developed and patented by Knoll "to create a crisp, tailored look with a clean silhouette, which prevented the fabric from shifting and bunching without traditional buttoning and tufting."[21] Knoll felt there was an inconvenience in the traditional method of buttoning (used, for instance, in the Barcelona Chair), as the buttons stuck out and offered the risk of catching the clothes of the sitter. Employing again a way of thinking related to the logic of tailoring—where it is common to work on the adaptation of an existing technique with the purpose of achieving a better, neater fit—she invented a unique solution to this problem.[22] In consonance with Florence Knoll's general design approach, the design of the Parallel Bar Collection worked toward the refinement of a programmatic feature. While in the Barcelona Chair Mies emphasized the structure, celebrating the technique of rolling and bending metal profiles, in the Parallel Bar Knoll worked on the seat, with the purpose of providing a more comfortable experience for the user. While placing the needs of the user came first here for Florence Knoll, adaptability was also in her agenda. "The Parallel Bar lounge chair could be covered in a wide variety of Knoll's upholsteries, offering a greater range of texture and color possibilities than the brown or black leather available for Barcelona chairs during this period."[23] (Fig. 7)

Florence Knoll defined her furniture designs as "architectural," to differentiate them from the "sculptural" pieces of the "architect-designed furniture in the Knoll line."[24] Through this description, "she asserted they were not simply meant for sitting on, but contributed to a broader vision of how an interior should function and how it should work with the building's architecture."[25] Her focus on the whole (interior) rather than on parts (furniture) was also evident in the way Knoll justified some of the desks she designed. "The desks emerged in many shapes," she wrote, "round, oval, boat-shaped and oblong *according to the plan*."[26] (Fig. 8)

Knoll liked to highlight that she designed furniture pieces not for artistic expression but to furnish her interiors when there was nothing else available to meet her needs. "Her furniture was meant to look unremarkable, but the sheer intention of its anonymity informs what unremarkability meant to her. For her, anonymity meant geometric form and carefully juxtaposed materials."[27] If, as an entrepreneur, Florence Knoll endorsed the exuberant and celebratory tone of many of the Knoll furniture designs, as a designer her attitude was different. She hid well under the shield of not knowing how to design furniture, in spite of the fact that her furniture pieces had a highly sophisticated—if subtle—level of design thinking. They were devised to blend rather than to stand out and they tended to be more considerate toward the needs of the user than the sculptural pieces of other Knoll designers. Playing down her vision with regard to furniture design meant that Knoll avoided the risk of clashing with designers she clearly had a lot of respect for, and probably wanted to remain on good terms with. It was, once more, a compromise, one that eventually had the detrimental effect of diverting the attention of the public and critics away from some of Florence Knoll's important design priorities.

The experimental approach to furniture design adopted by Knoll Associates, especially in relation to its "sculptural," more iconic pieces, required an equally exploratory handling of its production processes. When it came to hiring assistants to work on the Development Group—the team in charge of overseeing Knoll furniture production—instead of choosing engineers or technicians, Hans and Florence Knoll favored designers. Many of them came from the IIT Institute of Design in Chicago, which was at the time run by architect

Fig. 7: Parallel Bar Couch, by Florence Knoll, 1954, with chair and tables from the Pedestal Collection, by Eero Saarinen, 1957 (Courtesy of Knoll Archives)

Fig. 8: Boat-shaped Desk, by Florence Knoll, circa 1950s (Florence Knoll Basset papers, Archives of American Art, Smithsonian Institution)

Serge Chermayeff (with whom Hans had worked in London), and had Buckminster Fuller (1895–1983) as one of its tutors.[28]

Product development was another area in which the Knoll company excelled. Like in the other divisions of the company, this had a clearly established culture of showing a great deal of respect toward the design idea. As Knoll designer Vincent Cafiero explained,

> The original sketches of any design are alive. There's a spark, a freshness. As you interpret from sketch to production and then to the showroom floor, you can ruin the design. You can over-refine. You can lose the spark of the initial concept. There's an art to saying: cut off, this is it, this is all we're going to do.[29]

Florence Knoll was greatly respected as a design editor in the product development department. "She set the highest standards for herself and expected nothing less from those around her," declared Richard Schultz (b. 1926), who took part in the Knoll Development Group.[30] He also revealed that Florence Knoll revisited her architectural lessons when assessing the design of others: "She did her best conceptual work in two dimensions, and when the object for review was a chair, she would put the product prototype or mock-up on a table for review, 'to see it in elevation, as you would an architectural rendering.'"[31]

As well as working on product development alongside established architects and artists, some members of the Knoll Development Group worked as furniture designers themselves. Schultz and Don Petitt (1925–2003), for instance, both alumni from the IIT Institute of Design, not only had an instrumental role in getting Harry Bertoia's and Eero Saarinen's designs into production but also designed and produced their own chairs. Similarly, Warren Platner, the author of the remarkable Platner Collection, was an employee at Eero Saarinen's office when he got in touch with Florence Knoll with a view to produce his. His inspiration was, he said, Louis XV, and his orientation was toward "the gentle, the graceful, and the decorative," in contrast—he argued— with most Knoll designs of that period.[32] (See "Introduction," Fig. 2) Nonetheless, Platner felt he had a strong vision, and with his ambition and unique understanding of the Knoll approach he believed he could get an opportunity to take his idea forward.

> You hope to produce a classic. A classic is something that, every time you look at it, you accept it as it is and you can see no way of improving it. You can refine something forever, but you reach a point where you are moving backwards. Really strong things have a certain amount of awkwardness to them; otherwise they become weak.[33]

Platner's inspirations might have been different from Eero's, Bertoia's, or Mies's, but his approach, in reality, was not. Even though at first glance his collection may look more decorative than other Knoll furniture, it actually followed pretty much the same design principles. Like with other Knoll iconic designs—and in contrast with many of Florence Knoll's own furniture pieces—Platner's collection highlighted a beautified structure that celebrated the technical achievements of the day without, however, investing a great deal of effort in improving the experience of the seater.

No less crucial for the success of the Knoll vision were, of course, the factory workers. Hans Knoll chose southeastern Pennsylvania as the location of the first Knoll plant for a strategic reason. Most of the local population in this rural area of the US consisted of descendants of early eighteenth-century German immigrants. These people had no specific furniture-making skills, however Hans relied on their "Teutonic"

constitution and trusted that they would not disappoint.[34]
It turns out he was right. "They rose to the challenge: wood-
workers found their way to positions in the wood shop;
seamstresses became skilled upholsterers; handymen
learned the trade of furniture making."[35] Romantic as this
depiction of the beginnings of Knoll Associates may sound,
it also evidences Hans Knoll's discriminatory attitude. His
former employees reveal that, in other instances, he could
be manipulative and not very respectful:

> Hans was a guy who was extremely charming but could also
> be a bastard when he wanted to. In those days I don't think
> anyone thought about money because everybody loved Knoll.
> Most of them could have made more money someplace else,
> but Hans used to pat you on the back. You'd get to the point
> where you were going to quit, and he'd come and pat you
> on the back and you felt so great that he didn't have to give
> you a raise.[36]

Most of the Knoll team seemed to agree that Florence Knoll
was a more stable and reliable reference in the company—
thanks also to her great design flair. "Florence Knoll had
tremendous talent," said industrial designer Charles Pollock
(1930–2013). "I think there has never been a design director
in the world as well versed, competent, and as appreciative
of design with an artistic eye as she."[37] The furniture production of Knoll Associates in Florence Knoll's time is too
numerous to count. Apart from the work designed in house,
there were the pieces Knoll Furniture licensed, including
work by Franco Albini (1905–77) from Italy, Hans Bellmann
(1911–90) and Pierre Jeanneret (1896–1967) from Switzerland, and Antonio Bonet (1913–89), Juan Kurchan (1913–75),
and Jorge Ferrari Hardoy (1914–77) from Spain and
Argentina, who created the famous Butterfly Chair (1938),

Fig. 9: Knoll Associates advertisement featuring the Butterfly Chair, by
Herbert Matter, circa 1950s (Florence Knoll Basset papers, Archives of
American Art, Smithsonian Institution)

"one of the most imitated chairs in modern furniture history."[38] (Fig. 9) A great part of this work continues to be known,
to this day, without the acknowledgement of the extraordinary
role that Florence Knoll played in making all
of it possible.

In the beginning of Knoll Associates, Hans Knoll had
told Florence that he had the "ambition to develop a company
that need not struggle with established firms for an existing
market, but that would create its own market."[39] In the field of
furniture, the pair managed to achieve this by adhering to the
modern idiom, which turned the consumer's attention away
from some of the practical shortcomings of the Knoll products, concentrating instead on the quality of the design. The
argument the Knolls used was rhetorical. More than relying

on the practical, technical, and comfortable qualities of the products, it relied on the modern design ideas that could be associated with these products. For example, a press release created to communicate the introduction of some of Mies's chairs to the Knoll catalog reads:

> The importance of these pieces, aside from their distinctive appearance, is that they represent the design convictions of one of the 20th century's most important architects, who believed that perfection in detail and fine craftsmanship were essential to elegance. These pieces were designed not as isolated chairs or tables but as important parts of his most famous buildings.[40]

The text goes on to remark how "revolutionary" Mies's architecture was "with handling space," and how the "living-dining area in which the Tugendhat Chair and Brno Chair first appeared is still considered an important milestone in modern architecture."[41] A great part of the Knoll Associates' clientship was, as previously discussed, made of architects and other modernist enthusiasts who relished this type of discourse. Another part was formed of more ordinary people may not have known the references in the Knoll discourse but who— like the employees who worked in offices designed by the Knoll Planning Unit—were likely intrigued by the intellectual and cosmopolitan tone of their rhetoric.[42]

Knoll Furniture offered to the market the promise of an elegant, progressive, inspired lifestyle. The market strategy for Knoll Textiles was not very different. The previously mentioned use of tailoring fabrics, for example, was, first, a way to do something no one else was doing (and, hence, avoid the need to compete for a market, as Hans Knoll had originally intended). Second, it was a means for selling an aspiration— suits were considered to be elegant, respectable, worldly, and modern—as much as a product. (Fig. 10)

Fig. 10: Knoll tweeds, circa 1940s (Florence Knoll Basset papers, Archives of American Art, Smithsonian Institution)

Like Knoll Furniture, Knoll Textiles made a point of crediting its creators. "Some of the original designers were Marianne Strengell, director of weaving at Cranbrook, Anni Albers from the *Bauhaus*, [Antoinette Lackner] Prestini [later Webster, 1909–88] and Noémi Raymond [1889–1980]," Florence Knoll wrote in her collected papers.[43] Again, ordinary customers would not likely be familiar with those names, but the very fact they were mentioned was probably sufficient to impress.

Knoll's acknowledgment of the schools to which these textile designers were linked was also significant. The war period had seen plenty of activity in the textile departments of schools like the Cranbrook Academy of Art, Black Mountain College in North Carolina, and the IIT Institute of Design in Chicago. These were partially led by European immigrants, who, similarly to Hans Knoll, had come to the US to escape World War II and explore new ventures. Because of slow production and scarce materials, activity in the schools was driven by experimentation. This prepared the young designers to later cope with the changing demands and possibilities of the modern textile industry. "Hand-weaving at its best could and should be used as experimental laboratory material for mechanical production," declared Dorothy Liebes (1899–1972), an accomplished textile designer who was active during and after the war.[44] New, cheaper techniques of printing such as screen printing were also developed during these years (a consequence of a radical reduction in the use of copper printing rollers, so the copper could be repurposed for military use), and that added to the experimental and dynamic tone of the work.

When Knoll Textiles was officially founded in 1947, the general scenario was, however, no longer one of scarcity of techniques and materials, but rather one of excess of supply. In an article from 1945, Hans Knoll expressed a concern that the textile industry might be "flooded with ill-considered products" as a consequence of the "military developments in the war years."[45] With their unconditional enthusiasm toward technology, modernist advocates like Florence and Hans Knoll saw it as part of their remit to find suitable solutions for these developments and guide their applications in the civilian market. Hans had already tried to recycle war materials and technology in the first incarnation of the Planning Unit. Whereas his first attempt was unsuccessful, with Knoll Textiles the project proved to be fruitful. Knoll Associates' industry collaborators included Bridgeport Fabrics (automotive and aircraft) and Anchor Plastics Company, the Concordia-Gallia

Corporation, and the Chicopee Manufacturing Corporation (all producers of plastic webbing). "Knoll furniture appeared in advertisements for all of these companies, not only reinforcing Knoll's image as an innovative company interested in using modern materials, but also underlining the suitability of such materials for modern furniture."[46]

Florence Knoll related Knoll Textiles' adoption of innovative materials and techniques to demands from the design industry rather than as an effort to mitigate the excess of supply produced by manufacturers who had been active during the war.

> As I was coordinator of both furniture and fabrics, I gave very special attention to the suitability of fabrics in relation to furniture upholstery problems. We discovered the need for certain colors and textures and strength characteristics through the demands of the many kinds of jobs we worked on. This led to new designs which were added to the line. For example, transportation cloth was the result of General Motors' request for a tough fabric for Eero Saarinen's first moulded office chair. It took months of experiments to meet the exacting standards. We always maintained our quality standards from the Volkswagen to Rolls Royce quality. Any fabric that didn't measure up didn't survive.[47]

The above-mentioned Transportation Cloth—developed by designer Eszter Haraszty (1920–94), who had been introduced to the Knolls by her fellow countryman Marcel Breuer—consisted of a strong rayon yarn woven in a particularly tight structure and backed with latex for additional strength. This combination was intended to make this product very resistant to abrasion and suited to withstand heavy-duty wear. Haraszty proudly called it "the first industrial fabric—the first one that stood all the tests."[48] The reality was, however, that this textile initially caused many problems, as the rayon was highly susceptible to soiling and sun damage, causing the cloth to weaken and split. The manufacturer eventually solved the issue by creating a new version, the Nylon Transportation Cloth, which remained in the Knoll catalog until the late 1970s.

Weaves like the Transportation Cloth, of which Knoll Textiles produced an immense range, were particularly useful for upholstering "sculptural" furniture. "Simple non-directional weaves were especially important for chairs with compound curves," Florence Knoll wrote.[49] They also provided an elegant option for furniture with straight lines, as they highlighted the form and design of the piece. Naturally, the fact that textiles that celebrated technical innovation were a good match for furniture with a similar orientation was hardly a coincidence.

Scholar Susan Ward writes, "Knoll kept up with the latest industrial developments and was frequently one of the first companies to adopt a new fiber as it became available."[50] While some textiles, like Transportation Cloth, were produced for specific projects, others were more open ended. Evelyn Hill Anselevicius (1923–2003), a talented designer who had studied at Black Mountain College under Anni Albers, focused a great part of her time at Knoll Associates during the 1950s and the 1960s working on the development of highly experimental handwoven fabrics. Her pieces combined all sorts of materials—rayon, plastic, silk, mohair, fiberglass, and horsehair, along with more conventional yarns—pushing the techniques of weaving to such an extreme that some fabrics would not even hold together when they were cut. (Plate 10) Anselevicius's textiles were more popular with the press than with customers. Widely published in magazines, they slowly helped open the textile industry to new color and texture combinations.

Being experimental required Knoll Associates to have a bold attitude toward its clients and collaborators. Many Knoll textiles encountered serious challenges during production, to which the company's executives would respond candidly, saying that things "like this do happen if you work with new fibers. It does not mean that Knoll has supplied you with a bad product. This is all in the experimental stage."[51] Perhaps unsurprisingly, the idea that something might fail due to its innovative characteristics was not received so badly, especially by the architects who collaborated with the Knolls. They "got interested," Knoll textile director Suzanne Huguenin (1916–2008) observed, alluding to the enthusiasm many of the architects of the time expressed for all things related to technological innovation and experimentation.[52] Especially "in the textile department," she added, "we were almost amateurs, but that was probably the charm."[53] To many of Knoll collaborators, taking part in the company's cutting-edge discourse was so exciting that they seemed to be prepared to deal with eventual shortcomings. This shows how powerful the brand Hans and Florence created had become.

The Knolls were pioneers not only in terms of their technical research on textiles, but also in their commercial strategy. Florence Knoll noted, "We were regarded with suspicion in 'in the trade' but others followed suit in years to come." She was proud to remark that "Knoll was the first furniture company to become a textile converter."[54] Textile converters "purchase unfinished fabrics (called 'gray goods') and arrange for them to be finished (bleached, dyed, printed, and so on) to a buyer's specifications."[55] Converters may also, as Knoll Associated did in many instances, develop designs and find mills to manufacture them, or buy exclusive rights to designs that have been developed by a mill. In some cases, converters might work with multiple manufacturers for the production of a single textile (commissioning, for example, one mill to bleach or dye the fabric, and another to print it), selling it under their brand. The pioneering commercial approach of Knoll Textiles enabled Florence Knoll to have an even greater degree of control over the Knoll look. Producing fabrics in house meant she did not need to rely on the existing market to find the textiles to match her interiors: she could simply create them.

In consonance with the relative sameness of the Knoll look, the general style of the textiles produced and represented by Knoll Associates during the two decades of Florence Knoll's tenure in the company was remarkably uniform. In the weaves, colors generally ranged from the neutral (beiges, grays, and blacks) to the primary spectrum, with eventual variations to include browns and dark greens. Patterns were predominantly plain. (Plate 11) Anselevicius's "brilliantly exciting" use of "orange, purple, chartreuse and deep blue-greens" was certainly the exception rather than the norm in the Knoll vocabulary, and even these more extravagant colors were, in their majority, used in textiles that were predominantly plain and matte (bearing in this a close resemblance to the tailoring materials Florence Knoll used in her early work).

In the screen printing department, artists were guided toward simple and straightforward designs. Knoll's overall orientation was to move away from the "busy," "pictorial," "insistent," or "obtrusive" patterns popular at that time, as a reporter aptly defined them in a review of the Knoll Textiles first collection.[56] The technique of screen printing lent a casual feel to many of the company's products. For a textile named Fibra, for example—which would in time become a Knoll classic—Haraszty simply edited a photograph of the wire heddles of a loom. (Fig. 11) Many other Knoll prints were taken from photographs. Their look was predominantly abstract—and in many cases, like Fibra, self-referential— and their mood tended toward wit, play, and nonchalance.

Knoll Textiles produced a variety of casement cloth, see-through fabrics for window draperies. These were introduced by an English agent named Arundell Clarke, who directed the division for about a year from when it was first launched. Clarke sourced from a commercial fishing-net supplier a knotted linen webbing that Florence used as a curtain blind and room divider (and variations of it were used to hide equipment such as air conditioners). Years later, Anni Albers was one of the designers in charge of designing casement fabrics for Knoll Associates. She created many sheer textiles for the firm from the late 1950s to the early 1960s, sometimes naming them with evocative titles—like Rail, Lattice, and Track—that highlighted their abstract and structural (as opposed to ornamental) qualities. (Fig. 12) Some of Albers's designs presented technical problems and had to be discontinued, however others remained in the Knoll catalog for nearly twenty years, earning her regular royalties.

Knoll textiles—as much as its furniture and interiors— ranged in appearance from a chic and sober mood, reminiscent of tailoring fabrics (more noticeable in the weaves, including the casements) to a casual, fun feel (more perceptible in the prints). They capitalized on the notion of originality, argued through Knoll's design-oriented agenda as well as through its technical orientation. The Knolls claimed that their aim was "to fill a specific demand—to provide textiles appropriate for modern interiors and modern living."[57] Modern living required, according to the Knolls, a look that was cool, refined, irreverent, and practical, and that clearly demonstrated an alignment with technical innovation. With its highly edited vocabulary, it also excluded a whole range of possibilities in terms of human expression, sensibility and aesthetics.

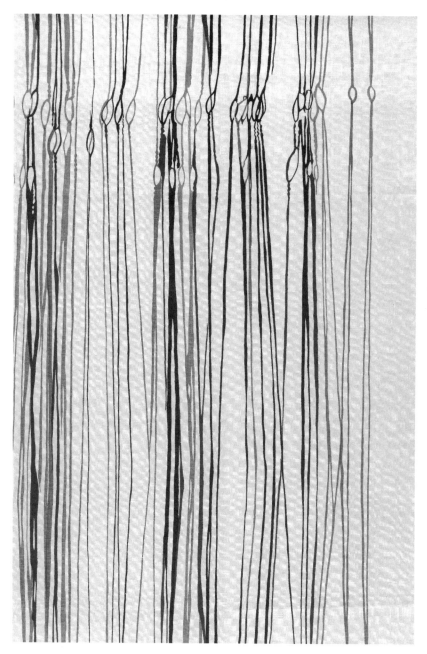

Fig. 11: Fibra Cloth, by Eszter Haraszty, 1953 (Cooper Hewitt, Smithsonian Design Museum, New York, NY, U.S.A., © Cooper Hewitt, Smithsonian Design Museum / Art Resource, NY / SCALA)

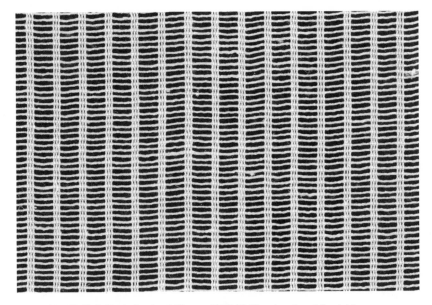

Fig. 12: Rail Cloth, by Anni Albers, 1958 (© The Josef and Anni Albers Foundation / Artists Rights Society [ARS, New York and DACS, London 2020)

With Knoll Textiles as much as with the other departments of the company, Florence and Hans Knoll were defining not only the style of furniture, textiles, or interiors. They were shaping the very idea of what form modern living should take. This included communicating to the modern individual—through their products and messages—what they were allowed to like, how they were expected to behave, and even who they were supposed to be. And the options for this individual were about as limited as the palette of colors and textures Knoll Textiles worked with.

> Even [the Knolls'] dog was ravishingly beautiful. His
> name was Cartree, and he was an enormous, enthusiastic,
> fluffy, and playful English sheep dog. I don't know who laun-
> dered him, but he, too, was impeccably groomed all of the
> time—quite an accomplishment in itself in view of the fact
> that Cartree spent most of the day asleep on a fire escape

Fig. 13: Sketch of Cartree, by Florence Knoll, 1946 (Florence Knoll Basset papers, Archives of American Art, Smithsonian Institution)

overlooking Sutton Place. When Hans and Shu and Cartree went out for a walk, they caused traffic jams.[58] (Fig. 13)

Cartree was an important figure at Knoll Associates. He was once on the cover of the Knoll Textiles catalog. A textile by renowned designer Marianne Strengell was named after him. And he also made appearances in *Vogue* and the *New Yorker*.[59] "Cartree enchanted everyone especially Herbert Matter [1907–84] who used him in our catalogues, brochures and advertisements," Florence Knoll wrote.[60]

Matter, the graphic designer in charge of the acclaimed Knoll ads from the late 1940s–1960s, found in Cartree the tone

Fig. 14: Cartree in a Knoll interior, by Herbert Matter, circa 1950s
(Florence Knoll Basset papers, Archives of American Art, Smithsonian
Institution)

of informality and coolness he thought appropriate to associate with the Knoll brand. Before working for Knoll Associates, Matter had collaborated with Charles and Ray Eames (with whom he shared a disposition for play and optimism) and had worked for the Swiss Tourist Office and *Arts & Architecture* magazine. Hans and Florence Knoll thought Matter had a special feeling for modern design. "Herbert was a quiet, unassuming and charming Swiss with a wonderful design ability," Florence Knoll wrote. "Everything was clear cut with imagination and even in some cases artistic whimsy."[61] Hans Knoll told the *New York Times* that the Knolls had appointed Matter for his ability to help their company build "an aura of leadership in contemporary design with an unspoken story."[62] The "unspoken story" Matter told in his ads was, generally, one of innocent play.

In a Knoll ad for the Butterfly Chair, Matter used pictures of his son playing on it. (See Fig. 9) As he recalled, he had come to the Knoll studio on a Saturday to photograph the piece, bringing the boy along. While he was preparing to shoot, his son started running around the chair, pretending to be a cowboy.

> I just let him do it and took pictures. We probably never said a single word; he just acted out a certain story he had in his mind…At first I thought I would just use the best images—the ones that were very special. Then I couldn't find them, so I used as many as I could get into two pages. I always find it a little dry to show pieces of furniture, so in each separate section I tried to find something to make the whole thing a little more alive.[63]

In another ad, Matter showed Cartree resting in an impeccable Knoll interior. (Fig. 14) The thinking in this one was jokingly counterintuitive: the image of a scruffy dog did not exactly sit naturally with the notion of selling refined furniture and textiles.

Matter's ads intensified the cheeky and sassy tone already present in some of the Knoll products. His work sometimes featured images of furniture taken from unusual angles, as well as furniture shown as it would be seen in an architectural drawing. Matter's work did not convey an obvious message. Rather than aiming to fall into the standardizations of the consumer market, it seemed instead to try to draw the consumer into the Knoll world. And the Knoll world, the ads implied, was as mischievous, playful, innocent as a child (or a dog).

In line with the optimism and playfulness of American mid-century culture, the Knoll Associates' graphic department produced imagery that was memorable and catchy, but that was also fundamentally disengaged and ultimately unaccountable from an ethical perspective. While Florence Knoll did not openly object to this position, she did not let herself be too carried away by it either.

NOTES

1. Larrabee and Vignelli, *Knoll Design*, 56.
2. Eliot F. Noyes, *Organic Design in Home Furnishings* (New York: Museum of Modern Art, 1941), 4.
3. See Brian Lutz, "Furniture: Form and Innovation," in Pelkonen and Albrecht, *Eero Saarinen*, 246-57.
4. Noyes, *Organic Design*, 5.
5. Ibid.
6. Ibid., 6; emphasis mine.
7. Ibid., 7-8.
8. Ibid., 11.
9. Architecture curator Cammie McAtee analyzes the Womb Chair mainly in terms of the psychological comfort it supposedly provides. Cammie McAtee, "Taking Comfort in the Age of Anxiety: Eero Saarinen's Womb Chair," in Robin Schuldenfrei, ed., *Atomic Dwelling: Anxiety, Domesticity, and Postwar Architecture* (London: Routledge, 2012), 3-25. Another account relating the modernist aesthetic to psychological and intellectual, as opposed to physical, comfort is Joseph Rykwert, "The Sitting Position: A Question of Method," in *The Necessity of Artifice* (London: Academy Editions, 1982), 23-32.
10. "Florence Knoll and the Avant-Garde," *Interiors* July 1957, 58-66.
11. Larrabee and Vignelli, *Knoll Design*, 69.
12. Ibid.
13. Larrabee and Vignelli, *Knoll Design*, 69.
14. In the meantime, Bertoia developed another design for the Knolls, the Bertoia Bench, which went into production in 1952. It was a simple design with welded wire legs that show "an early exploration of the material and foreshadows what was to follow." "Bertoia Bench," Shop & Browse, Knoll, accessed December 22, 2019, https://www.knoll.com/product/bertoia-bench.
15. Larrabee and Vignelli, *Knoll Design*, 57.
16. Ibid., 66.
17. For a more detailed account on the conditions of production of Mies's furniture designs in the earlier days of his career, see Schuldenfrei, "Subjectivity."
18. Lutz, *Knoll*, 33; emphasis mine.
19. Lutz, "Furniture," 254.
20. Tigerman, "'Heart and Soul," 195.
21. Ibid.
22. See, for example, Valerie Mendes, "Tailoring," in Amy de la Haye and Valerie Mendes, *The House of Worth: Portrait of an Archive 1890-1914* (London: V&A Publishing, 2014), 51-76.
23. Tigerman, "Heart and Soul," 195-9.
24. Tigerman, "Not a Decorator," 71.
25. Ibid., 70.
26. "Biographical Material," 24; emphasis mine.
27. Tigerman, "Not a Decorator," 71.
28. See Larrabee and Vignelli, *Knoll Design*, 150.
29. Lutz, *Knoll*, 55.
30. Ibid.
31. Ibid.
32. Larrabee and Vignelli, *Knoll Design*, 157.
33. Ibid.
34. Lutz, *Knoll*, 52.
35. Ibid.
36. See Larrabee and Vignelli, *Knoll Design*, 22.
37. Ibid., 157.
38. See "Jorge Ferrari Hardoy," Our Designers, Discover Knoll, Knoll, accessed August 14, 2019, https://www.knoll.com/designer/Jorge-Ferrari-Hardoy.
39. Byars, "No Compromise," 97.
40. "Knoll Introduces New Mies Designs," Press Release, circa 1950s (Knoll Archives).
41. Ibid.
42. For an account on how Knoll and other modernist products were integrated in the wider market, see Greg Castillo, *Cold War on the Home Front: The Soft Power of Midcentury Design* (Minneapolis: University of Minnesota Press, 2010).
43. "Biographical Material," 57.
44. Ward, "Design, Promotion, Production," 46.
45. Makovsky, "Knoll before Knoll Textiles," 89.
46. Susan Ward, "Making Knoll Textiles: Integrated Fabrics for Modern Interiors, 1945-65," in Martin, *Knoll Textiles*, 102-77, 104.
47. "Subject Files" (Folder 8, 4).
48. Ward, "Making Knoll Textiles," 140.
49. "Biographical Material," 57.
50. Ward, "Making Knoll Textiles," 153.
51. Ibid.
52. Ibid.
53. Ibid., 140.
54. "Subject Files" (Folder 8, 5).
55. Ward, "Design, Promotion, Production," 52.
56. Ward, "Making Knoll Textiles," 105.
57. Ibid., 173.
58. Blake, *No Place Like Utopia*, 171-72.
59. "Drawings, Sketches, and Designs" (Folder 3, 16).
60. Ibid.
61. "Subject Files" (Folder 8, 4).
62. William M. Freeman, "News of the Advertising and Marketing Field," *New York Times*, June 19, 1955, unnumbered.
63. Larrabee and Vignelli, *Knoll Design*, 117.

CHAPTER FOUR:
THE OTHER
FLORENCE KNOLL

"A crusher" is how Florence Knoll later described the Knoll Planning Unit.[1] In an article from 1984, almost twenty years after leaving the company, she said, "In a way I was bored. I worked so hard all my life, and I wasn't opposed to work; but really, when you've done 2,400 offices in the same building, it gets to be a bit much."[2]

She may have been disappointed with some of the criticism her last project for the CBS Headquarters received. For example, architecture critic Ada Louise Huxtable wrote, "The inside of the CBS is a solid gold corporate cliché; a lavish cocoon, complete to standardized concealed wastebaskets and accredited and almost as equally standardized abstract art."[3] Knoll Associates' designer Vincent Cafiero, a collaborator on the project, was similarly negative when he described one of his last days overseeing the CBS building. "I was in this white cubicle, looking across the street at other white cubicles, and in other directions there were other white cubicles. It boggled my mind what we were creating: we were creating little white boxes. It was a shattering experience."[4] The project also received some praise, with Knoll executive Cristina Rae, for instance, claiming that it had "made a spectacular exit" for Florence Knoll's "brilliant career."[5] Yet Knoll herself acknowledged her frustration with the commission, complaining that her design choices were limited because she was brought into the project "at the tenth hour":

> I had no time to develop any furniture or anything, and the planning was all done. The spaces, the ceiling heights, and the lighting were all pretty well set, and we were left with office partitions and office colors that had already been determined.[6]

Florence Knoll may have been a victim of her own success. The fact that she was the mind behind such a recognizable brand might have meant that she felt she was too closely associated with it to be able to reinvent herself in the public eye as a designer and entrepreneur. That might have played a role in her decision to retire so early, aged only forty-eight.

Her journeys, personal and professional, had been anything but smooth. Hans died, prematurely, in 1955, when Knoll Associates was at a peak, leaving Florence suddenly in charge of the entire business.[7] "I became president of the company with my usual emphasis on all phases of design leaving the business matters to others."[8] Even when Hans was around, notwithstanding the glamour the couple exuded, their personal relationship could be rocky at times, according to some accounts. A journalist reported, for instance, that Hans's "incessant womanizing" once provoked Florence Knoll's "moving out of their townhouse on Sutton Place, only to return shortly afterwards."[9] It must have been difficult to conciliate these personal matters with their sharing Knoll Associates.

Three years after Hans died, in 1958, Florence Knoll married Miami banker Harry Hood Bassett. They had met when the Planning Unit designed the interiors of the First National Bank of Miami, where Bassett worked. After their marriage, Knoll started to divide her time between New York and Florida. In 1960, she sold Knoll Associates, leaving the presidency yet retaining her original role as design director. In her resignation letter from 1965, Florence Knoll indicated that "her life outside of Knoll—her personal interests and the responsibilities of her private life, as well as her evolving independent professional life—was claiming more of her time, leading her to 'step out of my present relationship with Knoll Associates.'"[10]

Not much of her "evolving independent professional life" appeared, however, in publications or in her collected papers. Knoll reported that she worked as a consultant to the interior department of Skidmore, Owings and Merrill on a project for Southeast Bank (former First National Bank of Miami, where her husband Bassett was a chairman) in Miami, performing a role "not unlike my former role at the Knoll Planning Unit."[11] In an interview, she referred to her design of the interior of a boat—for her new family's use, it seems. And her designs for two private residential projects for herself and her husband, one "on a peninsula in Biscayne Bay and the other in a mountain valley in Vermont," appear in her collected papers.[12] It is intriguing that, despite the fact that Florence Knoll continued throughout her life to receive requests to take part in events and give interviews relating to her role at Knoll Associates, the press never took much interest in her later design production. If reporters brought curiosity and respect to the work of the "first lady of the modern office" in her younger years, they gradually reduced the more mature Florence Knoll to an upper-class housewife who wore emeralds "casually," worked at her own leisure, played tennis with her wealthy husband, and had lunch "served on a tray by the pool."[13]

The fact that Florence Knoll's contribution to Knoll Associates has rarely been interrogated critically may relate to the general lack of interest in her later work.[14] Her mission had been accomplished by the time she retired, it might be assumed. Knoll's later projects were also rather small in

Top, Fig. 1: Living room, Knoll Bassett House 1, Coral Gables, Florida, by Florence Knoll, circa 1970s (Florence Knoll Basset papers, Archives of American Art, Smithsonian Institution); **Bottom, Fig. 2:** Living and dining rooms, Knoll Bassett House 1, Coral Gables, Florida, by Florence Knoll, circa 1970s (Florence Knoll Basset papers, Archives of American Art, Smithsonian Institution)

Fig. 3: Entrance to bedroom with antique Spanish door, Knoll Bassett House 1, Coral Gables, Florida, by Florence Knoll, circa 1970s (Florence Knoll Basset papers, Archives of American Art, Smithsonian Institution)

comparison to the thousands of offices and extensive show-rooms she designed in her Knoll Associates years. Significantly, her new work was, as well, domestic, and for this reason it was more closely linked to the sphere of femininity to which Knoll managed to dissociate herself from at Knoll Associates.

It is revealing that in her later projects Knoll started to distance herself from an orthodox modernist vocabulary and play more freely with other references. This design work indicates a change of heart on Knoll's part, whether conscious or not. It may for this reason be understood as a self-critical interrogation of her own design attitude during the Knoll Associates years.

The design language of Florence Knoll's Knoll Bassett House 1 (circa 1970s) took up more or less where she had left at Knoll Associates.[15] Its layout is formal and its furniture modernist, with Knoll's usual precision and skill in making use of built-in storage and special fixtures (the ceiling, made of thin strips of wooden slats, is a special touch). Knoll displayed artworks and plants carefully throughout, and here and there she included some iconic historical pieces—like a ten-foot-high antique Spanish door that led to her bedroom and a large Teniers tapestry in the living room. (Figs. 1-3) The color scheme explores further the browns and greens from the CBS Headquarters, but the overall atmosphere is warmer. There is less emphasis on the modernist look and more free-dom in mixing pieces from different periods for the sake of creating a comfortable, elegant, personal setting.

> The 25' x 25' dining room was planned to be comfortable for two or a large crowd. We accomplished this by using boxed trees on rollers to add or subtract from the space. The free standing cabinet provided storage space and a serving counter. It also blocked the view of the kitchen and pantry doors. It was designed to provide a frame for an 18th Century tapestry by *Teniers*. It had been in the Bassett family. Because of its size (10' x 18'), the room was planned for it. The concealed lighting gave it a beautiful glow. The supplemental light came from the two reflecting pools, the round pool in the courtyard and candle-light. Additional pedestal tables were stored in a room nearby.[16]

It is interesting that Florence Knoll writes about adjusting the settings for different domestic activities—dining alone with her husband, or with guests; using candlelight to change the mood of the room—for this would be a type of discourse more associated with the concerns of a decorator than of a designer. If Knoll managed to divorce herself from the stereotypes surrounding femininity during her Knoll Associates period, in the houses she designed for herself they somehow became inescapable. Here she discusses an influence on her design for Knoll Bassett House 2:

> The early Vermont farm houses were built with 45 degree pitched tin roofs and narrow horizontal siding walls in red or yellow with white trim or white with black shutters and trim…We wished to maintain the general character but to still have a modern house with large glass areas for the view. By using post and beam construction we maintained the general form of the buildings, but recessed the glass areas from the south view back from the frame to retain the original form.[17]

This is Florence Knoll's first known description of her intention to actively engage with a design project's physical context, rather than to conceal inherent irregularities in order to fit the modernist sense of rigor; or to use them as eccentrical touches to an otherwise orthodox approach. A sketch for this project shows her idea for the living room of the guest house with a large sliding "barn" panel. (Fig. 4) The built interior, shown in photographs, bore a close resemblance to the original sketch. (Fig. 5) With walls fully clad in timber, the living room defines a casual atmosphere reminiscent of nautical design. In all three parts of Knoll Bassett House 2 (main house, guest house, and tennis barn) the design language was clear, but understated. (Fig. 6)

There is a personal, autobiographical tone in Knoll's design choices for this project, which is evidenced in some details. For example, she revealed that she chose an "antique capstan from a ferry boat" as a table base to work as "a

Top, Fig. 4: Sketch of guest house, Knoll Bassett House 2, Cambridge, Vermont, by Florence Knoll, circa 1980s-90s (Florence Knoll Basset papers, Archives of American Art, Smithsonian Institution); **Bottom, Fig. 5:** Living space of guest house, Knoll Bassett House 2, Cambridge, Vermont, by Florence Knoll, circa 1980s-90s (Florence Knoll Basset papers, Archives of American Art, Smithsonian Institution)

Fig. 6: South view of the guest house reflecting the mountains, Knoll Bassett House 2, Cambridge, Vermont, by Florence Knoll, circa 1980s–90s (Florence Knoll Basset papers, Archives of American Art, Smithsonian Institution)

Fig. 7: Florence Knoll and Eero Saarinen with a prototype of the
Pedestal Chair, by Eero Saarinen, 1957 (Florence Knoll Basset papers,
Archives of American Art, Smithsonian Institution)

Fig. 8: "Antique building ornament detail," Knoll Bassett House 2, Cambridge, Vermont, by Florence Knoll, circa 1980s–90s (Florence Knoll Basset papers, Archives of American Art, Smithsonian Institution)

counterpoint to the [Eero] Saarinen dining table at the other end of the room."[18] With this pair, she paid tribute to her old friend Eero, alluding to their early days at Knoll Associates, when they collaborated with a boatbuilder to make prototypes for the Womb Collection. (Fig. 7; see also Plate 3) "[The boatbuilder] was very skeptical," she recalled. "We just begged him. I guess we were so young and so enthusiastic that he finally gave in and worked with us. We had lots of problems and failures until they finally got a chair that would work."[19]

In her papers, Knoll prided herself for having rescued a "weather vane from the Wells Cathedral in England" to use in this house. She also includes in her notes and photos of Knoll Bassett House 2 details of ornaments that seem to have no reason for being there apart from the fact that she simply liked them.[20] (Fig. 8) Knoll's attitude for this design is clearly more relaxed than that of her discourse from the Knoll Associates years. Her approach is less rigorous. It is clear as well that

Fig. 9: Tennis barn of Knoll Bassett House 2 under construction, Cambridge, Vermont, by Florence Knoll, circa 1980s–90s (Florence Knoll Basset papers, Archives of American Art, Smithsonian Institution)

Knoll enjoyed the challenge of working with an entire architectural structure rather than just its interior, as she includes some beautiful images of the construction of the framework of her vaulted tennis barn in her archive. (Fig. 9)

The bric-a-brac in Knoll's Vermont home as well as its autobiographical quality invite comparison with the work of other well-known female designers, like Ray Eames, Lina Bo Bardi, and Alison Smithson. (Plate 6) They also relate to the cult of the interior from which, many authors claim, a specifically feminine design culture (a culture that the modern movement went to great lengths to ridicule and trivialize) was starting to emerge.[21] The problem with this reading is that this so-considered feminine design culture is too deeply entwined with the stereotype of a passive woman: alienated within the realm of the domestic, disconnected from reality, and, as discussed in Chapter One, prone to fantasy and day-dreaming. The main social role of this woman, as historian Penny Sparke explains, is one of a "beautifier."

> A chandelier could be described as "delicate," an epithet
> long associated with femininity and the female body. For the
> Victorians, these feminine attributes were considered to be
> "natural" features of the female sex, a result of her essential
> and physical characteristics. Beauty, it was generally agreed,
> was a fundamental attribute of women and, therefore, women,
> rather than men, were ideally qualified to inject it into the
> domestic setting.[22]

Confronted with this depressing scenario, it is hardly surprising that many female designers working in the early twentieth century—Florence Knoll included—grew rather allergic to the values and sensibilities associated with the so-considered feminine culture of their time. As a consequence, they embarked fully on the modernist critique of all aspects related to it.

Irish designer Eileen Gray, for example, influenced by the writings of Adolf Loos (1870–1933) and Le Corbusier, started to resent her own early decorative pieces, "which she considered too individualistic" (an attribute closely associated to the stereotype of the alienated woman).[23] Gray became uncomfortable, her biographer Peter Adam revealed, with the "fascination with surface effect" that had characterized her work in the first two decades of the twentieth century (again, surface and superficiality bore close connections to early twentieth-century ideas of femininity).[24] She started to look, instead, for "cleaner forms and low-cost materials, for naturalistic geometrical surfaces, decorated with simpler elements such as handles made from bones."[25] Gray's shift in style also implied a renunciation of the Eastern inspirations that had been a strong feature of her early work. For Gray, the sense of rigor established by the modernist discourse was incompatible with many forms of social and cultural inclusion.[26]

The modernist condemnation of what was regarded as an essential part of the economy of femininity and feminine taste also entailed a disapproval of certain aspects of human sensibility—delicacy, for instance—that are, obviously enough, not exclusive to women. Modernism aspired to shape not only our environment, but also our identities. The human ideal it advocated was one deprived of memory, nostalgia, and sentimentality. Correspondingly, many modernist female designers promoted their work as well as their own personalities as progressive, forward-looking, and essentially unsentimental. Florence Knoll criticized Hans Knoll's and Jean Risom's "romantic" taste. Ray Eames stressed she had a more "abstract," and "anti-ornamental" artistic inclination than her husband Charles.[27]

The trend stuck. In a recent publication on designer Charlotte Perriand, she is described "as the very symbol of the resolutely and definitely contemporary woman: intrepid, free, audacious, independent, sporting."[28] Perplexingly, female designers came to be praised for having traits that actually match those more conventionally associated to masculinity and sometimes even to the more extreme stereotype of the alpha male. In another fairly recent publication, Lina Bo Bardi was described by her biographer Zeuler R. M. de A. Lima as a woman who "took pleasure in seducing but not in being seduced."[29]

Modernist female designers contributed actively—although perhaps unknowingly—to the shaping of alternative stereotypes of femininity, including the one of the "working woman": rational, grounded, dutiful, emotionally robust, rigorous, and dynamic. These new stereotypes, seemingly

defined as the exact opposite of the old ones, were nevertheless just as reductive. Writing about the role of professional
women in the corporate environment of the early twentieth
century, scholar Angel Kwolek-Folland remarks that, at the
time, an idea of an overtly devoted and competent female
employee emerged. Somehow paradoxically, she explains,
this idea reinforced the "image of women as symbolic house-
keepers, governing the tempers of messy, childlike men,"
and emphasized "the traditional definition of women as
wives, mothers and homemakers."[30]

The notion of the faultless worker resonates with the
"meat and potatoes" role Florence Knoll took at Knoll
Associates: filling in the gaps and keeping the house in order
while others could be more playful and experimental. This
might explain why, in her case, fitting into a modern feminine stereotype did not prevent her from also being associated, later in her life, to a traditional one (the housewife who
decorated her own house, wore emeralds, and ate lunch by
the pool).

If in the earlier stages of her career Knoll had abided to
values associated with the early twentieth-century culture
of femininity— when designing, for instance, bespoke curtains for the CBS Headquarters and, more generally, when
acknowledging the important role interiors and textiles
played in architecture—she did this with extreme reserve.
Like other women designers of her time, Knoll partially boy-
cotted a freer, more inclusive, and more diverse design language and attitude, likely with the hope of extricating herself
from an unappealing feminine stereotype associated with
the activities of the interior decorator and the housewife. Her
strategy, nonetheless, backfired. Knoll ended up contribut-
ing to the dissemination of a design look that promoted the
discriminatory approach of modernism and, later in her life,
she became a victim of that very same discrimination.

Fig. 10: Knoll Showroom, 575 Madison Avenue, New York, by Florence Knoll/Knoll Planning Unit, photographed by Robert Damora, 1951 (Courtesy of Knoll Archives)

Whether Knoll's compromises were deliberate or not, she paid a price for them. Examining her career, one gets but a fleeting glance of how her design language might have evolved had she taken a stronger stance and done things more in her own way. While it is likely that this would have been very difficult at the beginning stages—her early Knoll Planning Unit commissions were conditional on her adopting the Bauhaus style—it seems that it might have been possible later had she used her influence to advocate for a different, more personal aesthetic. Knoll interiors could have been less standardized. Knoll furniture might have been less sculptural, more tactile. And the overall orientation of the company would probably have verged more toward subtlety and tactfulness than toward playfulness and wit. Florence Knoll might have contributed more to the consolidation of a feminine design culture had she not restricted her style so strongly to modernist standards. Most certainly, however, her style would have never conformed to any stereotype of femininity. For stereotypes are artificial constructions that tend toward oversimplification, and Knoll's personal identity and design approach were anything but simplistic.

"Part of modern architecture and design's historic and lasting allure was its connection to luxury," wrote architectural historian Robin Schuldenfrei.[31] Florence Knoll's designs remain influential to this day, owing extensively to their connection to wealth and success. Evidence of this may be found in the settings of the recent American television series Suits, set in the late 2010s. In *Suits*, Knoll-inspired interiors feature as backdrops for multimillion dollar deals handled by an impossibly smart team of professionals from a fictional New York City law firm. Interiors, clothes, shoes, hairstyles, and even dialogues are as sleek as they get. In *Suits*, style and affluence go, unquestionably, hand in hand.

Just like Florence Knoll wished, the Knoll look did become a classic, and it came to encompass some of the highest desires and aspirations of modern and contemporary life. If she was responsible for disseminating the trend, she was not the one who started it. Knoll's design at its most luscious was directly influenced by the work of Mies van der Rohe—most notably by the interiors he designed while he lived in Germany in the first half of the twentieth century, many in collaboration with interior, exhibition, and furniture designer Lilly Reich.[32] Luxury, in Mies's designs, was expressed through diverse means. They included "technical virtuosity," which called for ambitious structural solutions and originated large, generous, light spaces in stark contrast to the much more crowded and dark pre-modernist interiors; the "showcasing of new materials," for example, nickel and chromium plating; the use of "traditional materials newly deployed for modernism," for instance, travertine, marble, and onyx—but also velvets, leathers, and silks.[33]

> Rather than using materials to express concepts of mass production, industry, or technology, Mies's materials were statements of modern elegance and luxury. The social status and taste of Mies's clients was reflected in his choice of elite materials for their dwellings, illustrating the ways in which objects, through their materials, could be aligned with subjects. It is without question that this had always been the case with regard to an elite clientele and their architectural representations, from Louis XIV's Hall of Mirrors at Versailles to Karl Fredrich Schinkel's pavilion at the Schloss Charlottenburg.[34]

Knoll's interiors made use of similar indicators of opulence, albeit generally they were employed in a slightly more modest fashion. Mies and Knoll made use of an old architectural trope when they employed sumptuous materials in their

Fig. 11: Barcelona Pavilion, by Mies van der Rohe and Lilly Reich, photograph by Erich Lessing, 1928–9 (Licensed by SCALA / Art Resource, NY)

interiors. In addition to conveying the sheer elitism of their designs, they imbued their ambiences with a theatrical atmosphere, echoing the traditional interiors from which they took inspiration. Writing about the Knoll Showroom she designed in Chicago in 1953, Florence Knoll remarked that it "was basically a black void delineated by a white frame with floating white ceilings and light wood panels. The furniture groups were flooded with pools of light within the black void."[35] Quite literally, the showroom was devised like a theatrical stage: a black box with "pools of light" directing the eye of the beholder to the relevant scenes, so to speak. (see "Chapter 1," Fig. 26) The theatrical, dramatic quality of Mies's and Knoll's interiors suggests that these designs had a message to convey.

A case in point is Knoll's 575 Madison Avenue Knoll Showroom, in New York, from 1951. (Fig. 10) Apart from displaying furniture in an impeccably curated setting, this interior also featured a small pond. Knoll described this as a lily pond used as a space divider in her collected papers.[36] Knoll may well have been influenced by the design of another, much more substantial and imposing, pond at Mies and Reich's Barcelona Pavilion. (Fig. 11) The ideas evoked by these two elements could not, however, be more different. While the bronze statue in the Barcelona Pavilion pond commemorated the traditional (and condescending) idea of the woman as muse, the lilies from the Knoll Showroom related to a more complex narrative.[37]

> Water lilies (and related members of the Nymphaeaceae family, such as the lotus) held an important place in numerous cultures and religions. The word "lotus" comes from the name of a nymph, Lotis, who, as Ovid writes, turned into a water lily while fleeing from Priapus's vile pursuit.[38]

The water lily refers, in Ovid's myth, to a goddess who escaped an attempted rape. While referencing, whether intentionally or not, Mies and Reich's Barcelona Pavilion with a pond, Knoll significantly averted the trap of providing a frozen representation of an ideal female figure. Instead, she presented a metaphor that quietly challenged conventional stereotypes of femininity. Features like the lily pond point to a talent that Florence Knoll did not fully develop in her practice: her ability to play with narrative and myth and, through this, potentially defy rooted beliefs and assumptions. It is regrettable that, in spite of all her success and achievements, Knoll has not had a chance to explore these more nuanced aspects of her language further.

NOTES

1. Chusmir, "Florence Bassett's World," 28L.
2. Maeve Slavin, "Aesthetic Revolutionary," *Working Woman,* January 1984, 78.
3. Tigerman, "Heart and Soul," 223.
4. Larrabee and Vignelli, *Knoll Design,* 134.
5. Ibid.
6. Tigerman, "Heart and Soul," 223.
7. Hans died, tragically, in a car accident while on a business trip to Havana.
8. "Biographical Material," 13.
9. Byars, "No Compromise," 98.
10. Lutz, *Knoll,* 68.
11. "Biographical Material," 84.
12. Ibid., 87.
13. Warren, "Woman Who Led Office," 40.
14. To my knowledge, two residential projects by Florence Knoll appeared in publications. The first was her first home in Miami, featured in an article from the *New York Herald Tribune.* And the second was an apartment, also in Miami, to which she and her partner moved in the 1980s, shown in *Vogue Decoration.* It seems that the above-mentioned properties served as permanent residencies to the Bassetts, while the two houses Knoll added to her papers were holiday or weekend homes. The articles praise the interiors for their connection with the Knoll look, and do not acknowledge the steps Florence Knoll took developing her design language after she left Knoll Associates. See Harriet Morrison, "Florence Knoll to Receive Award," *New York Herald Tribune,* April 25, 1961, 18; and Olivier Boissière, "Florence Knoll Bassett, Style's Ambassador," *Vogue Decoration,* Edition Internationale, no. 22, 1985, 145–46.
15. Knoll Bassett House 1 is recorded as "undated" in Florence Knoll's collected papers. In her "Letters," its address starts to appear around the mid 1970s, therefore I concluded that the house dates from this period (or, potentially, from an earlier date).
16. "Subject Files" (Folder 3, 5). The same tapestry features in a photograph of the Southeast Bank scheme, which dates from 1982 (see Figure 15, Chapter 2). On the back of this photograph, Florence Knoll wrote that "The Teniers Tapestry was later used in our house in Coral Gables [Knoll Bassett House 1]." ("Subject Files," Folder 21, 8). It is confusing that Knoll writes above that the living room of Knoll Bassett House 1, which dates from the 1970s (or before), was designed to fit the tapestry, and, in another source, she suggests the tapestry was only

moved to this house at a later date. Due to the limited amount of documentation available on the works Florence Knoll designed after she retired from Knoll Associates, it was not possible to clarify this issue.
17. "Subject Files" (Folder 4, 2).
18. "Subject Files" (Folder 4, 13).
19. Larrabee and Vignelli, *Knoll Design,* 56.
20. "Subject Files" (Folder 4, 6).
21. As discussed in the first chapter of this book. See, also, Penny Sparke, *As Long as It's Pink: The Sexual Politics of Taste* (Halifax, N.S.: Press of the Nova Scotia College of Art and Design, 2010); Mark Wigley, *White Walls*; and Janet Stewart, *Fashioning Vienna: Adolf Loos's Cultural Criticism* (London: Routledge, 2000).
22. Sparke, *As Long as It's Pink,* 16.
23. Peter Adam, *Eileen Gray: Her Life and Work* (Munich: Schirmer/Mosel, 2008), 64.
24. Ibid. On the topic of femininity and "surface effect," Bauhaus artist Oskar Schlemmer remarked, "Where there is wool, there is a woman who weaves, if only to kill time." Ulrike Müller, *Bauhaus Women: Art, Handicraft, Design* (Paris: Flammarion, 2009), 10. See also Parker, *Subversive Stitch.*
25. Adam, *Eileen Gray,* 64.
26. For a discussion of the problematic relationship of another female modernist designer, Charlotte Perriand, with the Japanese and other Eastern cultures, see Yuko Kikuchi, "Dialogue Between Cultures," in Sébastien Cherruet and Jacques Barsac, *Charlotte Perriand: Inventing a New World* (Paris: Gallimard, 2019), 270–307. Charles and Ray Eames also used many non-Western references in their work, which they described as "functioning decoration." See Pat Kirkham, *Charles and Ray Eames: Designers of the Twentieth Century* (Cambridge: MIT Press, 1995), 143–200. Their approach was to adopt a playful attitude when dealing with foreign elements, which emphasized their exoticness and otherness. Lina Bo Bardi was very interested in the Brazilian vernacular, however her point of view was not substantially different from the one of the Eameses. In contrast to the patronizing tone of the modernist discourse, in the nineteenth century interior, femininity was, as explained by architecture curator Juliet Kinchin, predominantly associated with the "French and Oriental styles," which were, in this

context, treated equally—non-hierarchically, and without affectation. See Juliet Kinchin, "Interiors: Nineteenth-Century Essays on the 'Masculine' and the 'Feminine' Room," in Pat Kirkham, ed., *The Gendered Object* (Manchester: Manchester University Press, 1996), 16.

27. See Pat Kirkham, "Humanizing Modernism: The Crafts, 'Functioning Decoration' and the Eameses," *Journal of Design History* 11, no. 1 (1998): 15–29.

28. Suzanne Pagé, "Introduction," in Cherruet and Barsac, *Charlotte Perriand*, 25.

29. Zeuler R. M. de A. Lima, *Lina Bo Bardi* (New Haven: Yale University Press, 2013), 22. The image of the seductive woman with which Lima describes Bardi relates to the stereotype of the femme fatale, another product of male fantasy. Elsewhere in the book, he addresses other aspects of Bardi's character, including her vulnerability. In another book, focused on her drawings, Lima in fact provides a much more detailed and accurate account of Bardi's complex identity. Using catch statements as the one above—which Lina Bo Bardi might, by the way, have approved of (for she was often more comfortable with the so-considered stronger aspects of her personality than with its more vulnerable and delicate features)—can however have the effect of encouraging a simplistic reading of Bardi's character and position. See Zeuler R. M. de A. Lima, *Lina Bo Bardi: Drawings* (Princeton: Princeton University Press, 2019). For another account on modernism and the masculinization of femininity, see Jordan Troeller, "Breuer's New Women," in Elizabeth Otto and Patrick Rössler, *Bauhaus Bodies: Gender, Sexuality, and Body Culture in Modernism's Legendary School* (New York: Bloomsbury, 2019), 311–32.

30. Kwolek-Folland, "Gendered Environment," 174.

31. Schuldenfrei, *Luxury and Modernism*, 269.

32. Mies's interiors of this period consisted largely of domestic settings, including the Tugendhat House in Brno, Czech Republic (1928–30) and the Esters House (1927–30) and the Lange House, both in Krefeld, Germany. They comprised, as well, some public buildings, such as the Barcelona Pavilion in Spain (1928–29). For an account on the collaborations between Mies and Reich, see Christiane Lange, *Ludwig Mies van der Rohe & Lilly Reich: Furniture and Interiors* (Ostfildern: Hatje Cantz, 2006).

33. Schuldenfrei, *Luxury and Modernism*, 157.

34. Ibid., 158.

35. "Subject Files" (Folder 13, 2).

36. "Subject Files" (Folder 12, 12).

37. On the problematic image of the woman as muse, see Griselda Pollock and Rozsika Parker, "Painted Ladies," in *Old Mistresses: Women, Art and Ideology* (London: I.B. Tauris, 1981), 114–33.

38. Ross King, *Mad Enchantment: Claude Monet and the Painting of the Water Lilies* (London: Bloomsbury Circus, 2016), 263.

AFTERWORD

Some of the pivotal events in Florence Knoll's life and career were triggered by chance. She might not have gone to Cranbrook had she not become an orphan at such an early age. She would, most certainly, not have become so close to the Saarinens. She might have even chosen a completely different career. Other equally decisive twists in her trajectory were defined by the circumstances of the time: her encounter with Hans, for example, and the start of their collaboration. As a female professional, Knoll would have stood out in an office like the one of Harrison & Abramovitz (they were a minority). And, also as a result of the cultural and social limitations of her time, she happened to be in charge precisely of the type of work Hans was in demand for: interiors. Florence Knoll was very resourceful. She responded well to her chance encounters, and she adapted brilliantly to the conditions imposed by the context in which she lived. She made the most of the world the Saarinens "opened" to her. She took the company Hans had started to a whole new level. Together, they promptly responded to the demands and opportunities they were confronted with, creating and developing the different departments of Knoll Associates with great vision, competence, and determination.

Responding to chance and context, however, only took Florence Knoll so far. It did not allow her to make fully informed choices with regards to how she might contribute to the discipline in which she operated. It did not enable her to challenge her culture in a more profound and meaningful way. She did take tentative steps in this direction. For example, she refused to align herself with the uncritical optimism conveyed by many of the products and messages of her company. She let herself be influenced by the then so-considered "minor" practices of fashion and textile design in her signature paste-ups. She promoted interiors as a respectable and dignified area of design. She focused on the sphere of the office when it was common practice for women in interiors to work exclusively on the realms of the domestic and leisure. Here and there, Knoll even engaged in design procedures that contested the gender-, race-, and class-biased language of modernism that she had otherwise adopted (when making details for ornamented curtains in the CBS project, when learning from designers Vidal and Sévigny, when flirting with autobiographical gestures in her private commissions). These moves remained, however, somewhat hesitant in the wider context of her career. They constituted the exception rather than the rule.

Knoll's influence in her time and today is not limited to the area of design. As previously remarked, the Knolls were well aware that they were producing not only furniture, textiles, and interiors, but also a shaping of the very idea of what "modern living" should look and feel like. Had Florence Knoll's stance been more openly stated and developed, the very notion of modern and contemporary living might have changed considerably—and likely for the better. Her attitude, however, was not uncommon. It wouldn't be so even by today's standards. It is hard to speak out when you belong to a group that is disenfranchised. It is even harder to articulate a clear position and create a project that is solid and consistent enough to make a difference, let alone take such a project to fruition. Florence Knoll made some reluctant moves. Her steps, if timid, may still provide valuable guidance and inspiration.

INDEX

Published by
Princeton Architectural Press
202 Warren Street
Hudson, New York 12534
www.papress.com

ISBN 978-1-61689-993-6

Editor: Jennifer Lippert
Designer: Natalie Snodgrass

Library of Congress Cataloging-in-Publication Data
available from the publisher.